A Meditative Journey with *Saldage*

Homesickness for a Place, a Time, a Person that Cannot Be

B. Catherine Koeford

Order this book online at www.trafford.com
or email orders@trafford.com

Most Trafford titles are also available at major online book retailers.

© Copyright 2009 B. Catherine Koeford.

Edited by E. Abraham

Note for Librarians: A cataloguing record for this book is available from Library and Archives Canada at www.collectionscanada.ca/amicus/index-e.html

Printed in Victoria, BC, Canada.

ISBN: 978-1-4251-3180-7

Our mission is to efficiently provide the world's finest, most comprehensive book publishing service, enabling every author to experience success. To find out how to publish your book, your way, and have it available worldwide, visit us online at www.trafford.com

Trafford PUBLISHING   www.trafford.com

North America & international
toll-free: 1 888 232 4444 (USA & Canada)
phone: 250 383 6864 ♦ fax: 812 355 4082

DEDICATION OF MERIT

TO E.V.A.

May you become acquainted with tranquil single-pointed concentration . . . those who seek wisdom through the lens of tranquility glimpse reality in the same manner as a lighted candle -- the light chases away that which is hidden within a darken closet's shadows. Insight, once risen, shines light into closed hearts and minds and keeps the gloom of ignorance at bay.

Reading is an exterior exercise;
meditation belongs to the interior intellect.
Prayer operates at the level of desire.
Contemplation transcends every sense.

~ Guigo

TABLE OF CONTENTS

Memory bridges our past with the present and brings us to an awareness that life is a cyclic process that demonstrates the opposite forces of togetherness and separation; therefore, this writing is but a reflection of a moment in this movement and of a self revisited while in this process.

I
INTENTION

THE THREE KEYS

I awaken to my in-breath. I sense the in-between. I release with my out-breath. I sense the in-between. I become mindful of my body and observing mind as they move in unison with the spirit of my breath.

I imagine myself in a forest of tall pine trees. Smooth river rocks and trimmed elephant grass edge a pathway covered with dark red, black, and gray colored gravel stones. The pine trees release their scent as they sway with the breeze. The singsong of birds fills the air as they flitter from one branch to another. Before me I see a clearing illuminated by the rays of the morning sun. As I step into the clearing, I feel warmth of the sun's touch and see a house centered within a field of harvest-ready wheat and question, "is this home?"

As I make my way through the wheat field, I find three ancient keys lying within a dust-filled furrow. Silver is the first key. A knowing tells me it opens a door to a space of tranquil abiding. Gold is the second key. It gives admission to a room of healing serenity. Diamonds make up the third key. It unlocks a keepsake of my remembrances.

The awakened groan of the wood planks welcome me as I step onto the weathered porch that surrounds the house. I find that the silver key fits the lock of an entryway door. Before I open the door and step over the threshold, I feel compelled to turn around and, with non-judgmental awareness, attend to and then put aside all that I see within and beyond the wheat field.

My consciousness rides upon my in-breath like a red kite riding upon the breeze traveling through a cloudless blue sky. It momentarily pauses in midair as my mind touches the in-between. Consciousness rides upon my out-breath like a white kite riding upon the breeze traveling through a cloudless blue sky. Again, it awaits in midair as my body senses the in-between. Together, consciousness, body, and mind move in unison with the spirit of my breath.

I step over the threshold and feel an inviting atmosphere of affectionate acceptance that encourages me to wander unencumbered throughout the interior of the house.

As a feeling arises, I welcome its arising. I acknowledge its quality (sadness, fear, joy, anger). I abandon its sensation; I sense its fading. I absorb its absence.

I find myself at the bottom of a stairway which I ascend. On the second floor I enter a room lightened by the light of the midday sun entering a picture window painted by the landscape that extends to where the blue ridge of the sky touches the earth's multi-green jagged horizon. Opposite to the window is a ceiling-to-floor bookcase lined with books, aged and worn. The warmth within this room embraces me with stillness, silence, and clarity. My eyes light upon a small trunk and I know that it is for me. As I pick up the trunk I find that it is light and fits with ease into the cradle of my arm.

As a feeling arises, I welcome its arising. I acknowledge its quality (sadness, fear, joy, anger). I abandon its sensation; I sense its fading. I absorb its absence.

I leave this room and again walk about the house. I find that the gold key opens a door to a central room of calm solitude. Stepping into this room I sense the presence of a compassionate being who introduces herself as Sophia, the aged guardian of the innermost things, "my heart hears the wordless tears and fears within your heart and feels the quiver of your heart-filled joys. You have entered the hearth of your home, an ancient site of healing."

As a feeling arises, I welcome its arising. I acknowledge its quality (sadness, fear, joy, anger). I abandon its sensation; I sense its fading. I absorb its absence.

I sit comfortably on the floor and open the trunk with the third key. As I explore the contents, I understand that they are mementos of my life's journey. My consciousness, mind, and body move in unison with the moment of my breath's spirit as I hold one keepsake after another. I acknowledge the memories, images, feelings that each memento evokes with the reminder that I am in a space of healing serenity and that I am not alone.

I feel a slight tugging within my heart as dark memories hidden within darker shadows accept the invitation to ride upon the in-breath of the compassionate guardian. With their departure, my body releases long-held tears. With my in-breath, I hear her whisper, "This is a time of healing transformation", and I feel a wondrous golden energy spread throughout my body.

As a feeling arises, I welcome its arising. I acknowledge its quality (sadness, fear, joy, anger). I abandon its sensation; I sense its fading. I absorb its absence.

A calling beckons me from beyond this house that feels like home. I hear permission to leave with a chosen remembrance or to place whatever arose back in the trunk. I step over the threshold; I feel an invitation to return whenever I wish.

The porch step invites me to engage in a mindful transition. My consciousness rides upon my out-breath like a white kite riding upon the breeze traveling through a cloudless blue sky. It momentarily pauses in midair as my mind touches the in-between. My consciousness rides upon my in-breath like a red kite riding upon the breeze traveling through a cloudless blue sky. Again, it awaits in midair as my body senses the in-between. Together, consciousness, body, and mind move in unison with the spirit of my breath.

The ancient wisdom of the hearth invites me to portray this meditation through a form of artistic expression of my choice; e.g., drawing, poetry, quilting, collage, needlework, story writing, painting, sculpture, gardening, weaving. I place my creation within the pages of this book.

Kalama Sutta

*Do not go upon what has been acquired by repeated
hearing, nor upon tradition, nor upon rumor, nor
upon scripture, nor upon surmise, nor upon axiom,
nor upon specious reasoning, nor upon bias towards
a notion pondered over, nor upon another's seeming
ability, nor upon the consideration 'The monk is our
teacher.'
When you yourselves know: 'These things are bad,
blamable, censured by the wise; undertaken and
observed, these things lead to harm and ill,' abandon
them.
When you yourselves know: 'These things are good,
blameless, praised by the wise; undertaken and
observed, these things lead to benefit and happiness,'
enter on and abide in them.*

~ The Buddha

About twelve years ago, I met a homeless woman who
identified herself as a sundowner. She described how each
evening's sun invited her to settle down along the side of
her life's path so that her journey could begin afresh in the
morning sun. She eloquently described an undercurrent of
yearning that ebbed and flowed throughout her soul and
how, in her past days, she found herself at the mercy of
private memories, thoughts, and imaginations and had
encountered, time and time again, various degree of
discontent despite the seemingly fulfilling qualities of her

life.

As I hear the suffering within women who story their lives through the multi-colored threads of substance use, I find myself acknowledging a similarity within each of these unique stories with my own metaphysical search for someone, something, or some place that remains beyond the forever next horizon. Each of our unique narratives reveal an unending wandering with satchels of discontent that tell of a spiritual emptiness and an emotional intimacy with a translation of the Brazilian word *saldage*, "a homesickness for a place one knows cannot be."

The governing aspect of the psychology within Buddhism is the investment to understand the roots of human discontent and to present a way of living that leads to the cessation of suffering. Within his speech, "Setting Rolling the Wheel of Truth", the Buddha identified four noble truths that begins with the acknowledgment and validation of suffering. From this starting point, he then identified the origins of our suffering. He furthered his understanding by noting that the easing of suffering begins as we let go of our relationships with the mental and behavioral qualities that are fed by greed, hatred, and ignorance and employ the guiding principles of wisdom, virtue, and diligence.

The last of the Four Noble Truths known as the Eightfold Path or Middle Way identifies the wisdom, virtue, and diligence that lead to social, psychological, kammic, and contemplative unity. These eight guiding principles extend beyond moral precepts to provide us with the tools to develop and maintain positive interpersonal relationships. They protect our minds from the internal turmoil of guilt and remorse as well as help us discover serenity and insight. They also bring us into harmony with the universal law of cause and effect. Lastly, they invite us to go beyond the *Golden Rule* "to treat others as *I* wish to be treated" towards a noble undertaking to honor the diversity of all sentient beings, "to treat others as *I and they* wish to be treated."

The Buddha's inclusion of the world "noble" in his discussion of "suffering" suggests a counter perspective to a Western presumption that those who suffer have been denied God's grace. Suffering through an Eastern lens is seen as an intrinsic aspect of life that is to be reverenced rather than a manifestation of something to hide in shame as if a consequence of moral discrepancy or a stain of original sin. Additionally, the "truths" of suffering and its cessation are presented as a reality that unlike a mirage does not deceive or disappoint.

The Kalama Sutta tells us that the Buddha wanted our truths to be known, not through the words of others, but through personal experiences as well as introspection and intuition. His words suggest that the way in which we comprehend and make sense of this vast and mysterious thing called life brings forth beliefs that have the power to either ease our discontent or intensify our suffering. Yet, to undertake, for one self, the challenge to analyze the mental ground one stands upon is to encounter a time of uncertainty. This uncertainty is like quicksand: its power to imprison will intensify in association with the struggle to escape the entanglements of concepts that formulate the foundation of one's life, family, culture.

Therefore, to observe, question, and analyze suffering through Buddhist psychology requires an acknowledgment that this endeavor will be influenced by the myths, beliefs, and expectations within my family of origin, how I understood doctrines within my religious upbringing, and the experience and training I have had as a psychotherapist.

Freud noted that suffering comes from three directions: the feebleness of our bodies, the superior power of nature, and more painful to us than that of any other, our relations with others. He also wrote, "In the last analysis, all suffering is nothing else than sensation; it only exists in so far as we feel it, and we feel it in consequence of certain ways in which our organism is regulated." The few who possess the ability to experience pleasure through special dispositions and gifts do not have "an impenetrable amour against the arrows of future."[1]

Those who are most likely to have intimate knowledge of what it means to be fettered to suffering are those who present with a history of chemical use, either personal, that of a significant other, or both. The dynamics within dependency resemble the autumn leaves traveling upon the surface of a stream; they are overt manifestations of the undercurrent that demonstrates how each of us seeks pleasure and will, in the long run, endure suffering if there is a thread of hope, no matter how short lived, of experiencing remembered pleasure. As Freud wrote: "The most interesting methods of averting suffering are those which seek to influence our own organism . . . The crudest, but also the most effective method people use to ease their suffering is through "intoxication [to] alter the conditions governing our sensibility so that we become incapable of

---

[1] Peter Gray, ed., *The Freud Reader* (New York, 1998), 730.

9

receiving unpleasureable impulses . . . The service rendered by intoxicating media in the struggle for happiness and in keeping misery at a distance is so highly prized. . . We owe to such media not merely the immediate yield of pleasure, but also a greatly desired degree of independence from the external world."[2]

This yield of pleasure and degree of independence that Freud identified creates its own attachment, which is compounded by an aversion to both the impermanence of intoxication and a re-engagement with life's discontent. Suffering intensifies as cravings and intrusive thoughts feed a desire to escape discontent. Therefore, a relentless ruminating and obsessing mind has the power to create as much suffering as physical dependence.

The Veranda

Women are empowered to step over the threshold of discontent and uncertainty within a trusting environment that encourages them to use their voice to speak of and process personal feelings, thoughts, and behaviors. Within all of us there are powerful emotions within our souls that remain voiceless and silent until they are conveyed through imagery and symbols. It is through creative endeavors - drawing, cooking, writing, painting, gardening, poetry, child rearing, photography, weaving, reading, work - that a woman may be able to give "voice" to that which words cannot convey.

All forms of art provide a means to help a woman

---

[2]Peter Gray, ed., *The Freud Reader* (New York, 1998), 730-35.

externalize that which silently moves her, to re-acquaint her self with self, to re-create a new awareness of self, to communicate about herself with others, and to meet her own wondrous feminine spirit/guide.

Stories, myths, and parables acknowledge and respect the unique individuality of each of us. Myths give voice, through their use of symbols, to what is hidden, unknown, or evasive. Stories that share the dynamics of human interactions silently plant a seed of personal truth in the dark component of each of us, waiting for the appropriate time to bloom and to nourish. They also illustrate the universal theme of suffering and its resolution. Parables, with their multiple levels of meaning, honor the unique perspective and understanding of both listener and speaker. These multiple layers of meaning touch what is salient to the reader and thus gift all readers with an invitation to define for self their own understanding, interpretation, and application.

The story of the Veranda provides an example . . . once upon a time in a peaceful village people would gather during the lunch hour to rest, eat their afternoon meals, and exchange village news and gossip. In the village square, some people chose to sit on the grass, others rested in the shade of a large tree, while some chose to sit underneath a century-old veranda. One afternoon without warning tragedy came to the village. Five people died and two were seriously injured when the veranda broke loose and fell to the ground. Before the end of the day, rumors, myths, and suppositions began to formulate from questions such as why that particular veranda? Why that particular day? Why that particular time? Why those particular people and not others?

These universal questions which have failed to ease suffering have given birth to myths of old.

It is my intention to illuminate my journey of homesickness using myths, stories, and poetry. I aspire to embrace this suffering with a mindfulness guided by the sublime seeds of compassion, loving-kindness, sympathetic joy, and equanimity. This journey through various Western and Eastern perspectives of suffering is being undertaken with a hope that I will define a healing-path that leads to an easing of a life ruled by discontent.

To heal does not mean to cure. To heal is a process of becoming whole and thus an invitation to see the world anew and to enter into a more gratifying connection with all that is life.

Nothing is hidden
It has always been clear as day
For divine wisdom; look at the old pine tree;
For eternal truth; listen to the birds sing;
Seeking the mind; there is no place to look;
Can you see the footprints of flying birds?
Above, not a single tile to shelter under,
Below, not a morsel of ground for support.

~ Zenrin

THERAPEUTIC EQUANIMITY

*Individuals have within themselves vast resources for
self understanding and for altering their self concepts,
basic attitudes, and self directed behavior; these
resources can be tapped if a definable climate of
facilitative psychological attitudes can be provided.*

~ Carl Rogers

I am acquainted with a mind filled with multiple crosscurrents of unfinished thoughts, stifled emotions, and passing moods. There is also a growing recognition that at times I am overwhelmed by discursive thoughts that are formed by habitual ways of thinking, led by my own various prejudices, impacted by personal preferences or aversions, colored by laziness or selfishness, and intensified by faulty or superficial observations. Sometimes I awaken to myself to find that while engaged in a behavior, my mind has entered a dreamlike state, and therefore events and conversations are vague and fragmentary. Sometimes I acknowledge this process or attribute it to boredom, anxiety, doubt, impatience, exhaustion, misjudgments, and self-salient triggers.

The practice of tranquility meditation assists me with my intention to be present with a client. It provides me with a tool by which to create an internal quiet space that allows for the clarity of mind that is a precondition for intuition and insight. This quality of quiet space within my being creates a likewise environment for the client to be with whatever arises during our session.

I have at one time or another within the therapeutic

environment experienced dynamics similar to those of meditation. Somehow, something hooks my attention away from the object of my attention, the client, and I find that for some unknown period of time my stream of consciousness has taken me from one thought to another. I have also found that my own emotional reactions, discriminatory thoughts, or self-reflective moods require an intentional silent nod of acknowledgment as I shift my focus to present moment.

To engage with a client through Rogerian concepts of accurate empathy, unconditional positive regard, and congruence requires the removal of the same five mental hindrances that block one's own meditative practice. To engage absent of these hindrances is a means by which to protect one's self from engaging in unethical behaviors and thus in protecting myself I protect the client.

> *Protecting oneself, one protects others; protecting others, one protects oneself . . . And how does one, in protecting oneself, protect others? By the repeated and frequent practice of meditation.*
> *And how does one, in protecting others, protect oneself? By patience and forbearance, by a non-violent and harmless life, by loving kindness and compassion." But self-protection is not selfish protection. It is self-control, ethical and spiritual self-development.*
>
> ~ The Buddha

Every healing intervention is motivated by suffering and hope - be it of the individual, family, friends, or a community agency. The value within suffering is that it contains a message of incongruence that awakens the motivation to heal. William James wrote that life is the manifestation of behaviors that attempt to avoid, overcome, or remove that which is seen to block us from that which we desire.[3]

The discontent that is presented during the initial meeting with a therapist very often times is colored by, and hidden under, numerous layers of attempts to ease pain. Therefore, what occurs within the isolation of suffering is a compounding of the original problem. Overcoming the defenses that shield one from acknowledging suffering requires a presence similar to how a person standing beside a pure, limpid, serene pool of water contemplates the reflected surface images, observes the life within the water's current, and notes the sediment's composition; to do otherwise only serves to fortify protective shields such as rationalization, minimizing, justification, or defiance.

With this in mind, it is my purpose as a clinician to engage with a client so that together we identify the origins and entanglements of the presenting concern, awaken the motivation to ease discontent, and then identify therapeutic goals that are congruent with the client's values, guiding

---

[3] William James, *The Principles of Psychology*, (New York, 1890), 7-8, "Romeo wants Juliet as the filings want the magnet; and if no obstacles intervene he moves towards her by as straight line as they. But Romeo and Juliet, if a wall be built between them, do not remain idiotically pressing their faces against its opposite sides like the magnet and the filings, Romeo soon finds a circuitous way, by scaling the wall or otherwise, of touching Juliet's lips directly. With the filings the path is fixed; where it reaches the end depends on accidents with intelligent agents, altering the conditions changes the activity displayed, but not the end reached; for here the idea of the yet unrealized end cooperates with the conditions to determine what the activities shall be."

principles, and moral guidelines. It is postulated; therefore, that the effective resolution of presenting concerns within a therapeutic environment requires a relationship that intentionally begins with the comprehension and acceptance of one's discontent "as it is."

"As it is" initiates a settling of internal criticism and disturbing feelings similar to the descent of sediment within a pot of muddy water. Consequently, to simply listen to a feeling, belief, or behavior "as it arises and as it is" is believed to be an effective way to begin a process of unraveling entanglements of thoughts, emotions, and actions. It silences troublesome intrusions and invites accurate empathy, congruence, and unconditional positive regard into the environment. Thus both the client and therapist are invited to emerge from their various shadows of anxiety, anger, grief, cravings, and confusion into a space of mindfulness.

Mindfulness is a non-judgmental and non-distracted presence that remains in the moment, moment by moment. This congruent presence is a prerequisite for the "letting in" and "being touched by the other" that is the essence of therapeutic empathy. What is not often acknowledged is the courage it takes for both client and clinician to allow their defenses to fade in order for empathy to awaken as "being touched" has the potential to awaken each person's vulnerabilities, loneliness, sadness, anxieties, shame, regret, anger, etc. Yet, when the barriers come down and the elements of mindfulness, empathy, and courage unite, a therapeutic environment is filled with creative, active, sensitive, and compassionate exchanges.

Freud discussed a listening technique in which the

attention is not directed towards anything in particular and is maintained with an evenly suspended attention to all that is presented. This manner of listening avoids the downfall of deliberate attention in which the listener is being guided by her own expectations or inclinations and thus selects what to listen for and what to disregard. Freud noted that when we follow our expectations, we will not hear anything but what we already know; and if we follow our inclinations, we will certainty falsify what we may perceive. "It must not be forgotten that the things one hears are for the most part things whose meaning is only recognized later on."[4]

It is my perspective that my role in the therapeutic environment is to listen, respond, and reflect upon what I hear, feel, observe, and imagine so that a client will sense, maybe for the first time in her life, that she is heard and understood. Through this process of validation, her experiences, myths, beliefs, perspectives, feelings, and memories are reflected back to her with a mirror of lessened anxiety, judgment, and reactivity.

The personal story is a narrative of our unique sense of identity. We create our identities through the stories we weave onto a tapestry that is formed against the background of our family mythologies. We pull threads from of an assemblage of recalled details from our pasts and weaved them into images that cast us in whatever role corresponds with our current situations, feelings, thoughts, or actions. The colored threads of this tapestry are often re-embroidered to reflect the creative and dynamic process of our perspectives as we shift in, out, and between various roles, feeling states, and cognitions. As we reflect on our

---

[4] Peter Gray, ed., *The Freud Reader* (New York, 1998), 357.

self-created images we are in turn affected by them; therefore, there is an unconscious re-weaving of our tapestries.

Our self-stories as well as our family mythologies create and maintain our identities and thus influence how we anticipate experiences, act, and subsequently interpret our situation. Becoming aware of the tapestry and images we are creating frees us to review patterned behaviors, reframe our story through different colored concepts, and to release rigid interpretations.

While a person sits in a recovery group and labels her struggle with drug and alcohol as an "addiction", she has begun to free herself from the power inherent in long-held secrets. As she tells her story she is weaving a tapestry of images that validates the hidden stories within others and thus invites listeners to abandon their alienated shame, anxieties, confusion, and anger. When she labels the various demons within addiction she dwindles their power as she un-shields their false promises. At the same time, the power of detrimental thinking begins to dwindle as its unsubstantiated lies are confirmed within the stories of others.

Within such a supportive and non-judgmental environment, each is invited into a process of bare attention that is non-coercive as they uncover the seeds of their suffering and thus begin to strengthen their recovery with renewed energy. It is after a meeting during the quiet of one's alone time that each attendee begins a process of dismissing what is personally invalid, questioning harmful behavioral patterns, or replacing painful concepts with constructive meanings. They, through their own individual reflection, take what is helpful for them at the moment and let the rest flow away.

Through this process of externalization, validation, and reformation an individual is being invited to become other to herself as if she were the audience in a movie theatre watching her life story being retold on a screen. Consequently, a new relationship with the self is formed that lessens the suffering that comes out of subjective rigidity, alienation of self as "the only one", and attachment to shame and guilt.

This process of healing requires that I, as a clinician, be as a mirror absent of assumptions, labels, expectations, and personal concerns. Therapeutic grounding comes as I remain present to what ever arises within the therapeutic setting. It requires a period of preparation in which to shelve any personal or administrative concerns, to silence my discursive ramblings, and to bring my self into the moment so that "bare attention" can be given to an issue, "as it is." There is also a need for a discerning presence to note the arising, abandoning, vanishing, and disappearance of awakening personal themes within a client's narrative. In sum, a mirror cleared of disturbing or distracting thoughts opens the door by which to engage with nonjudgmental awareness and thus invite trust into our relationship.

Trust comes about as a client finds herself in the presence of listening that reflects the her life story, that is, her struggles, hopes, dreams, and obsessions with equanimity, nonjudgmental respect, and compassion. It arises when the goodness within her is held to be true alongside the faith that goodness is an important aspect of her well being. If I do not have trust and faith in the healing process, I will remain hidden behind a barrier of defenses, ill will, and postures of "you must change." My absence of trust will only serve to reinforce the emotional patterns that she has found to be ineffective and served to intensify her concerns.

Trust arises within the therapeutic environment through its fundamental foundation of confidentiality. Trust emerges when I am able to release my personal agenda and have the strength to block the various anxieties of managed health care, social agencies, family and friends, the legal system, and the agency itself that contaminate the therapeutic environment. Trust follows my ability to contain what is expressed and the intensity of the expression so that there is a safe place in which psychological transformation can occur.

Trust calls for me to provide a calm, soothing climate through my own ability to be grounded as well as provide space that is clean, open, and uncluttered. Therapeutic norms include an agreement between both of us regarding length of sessions, regularity of meetings, understanding and consistency of our roles, ethical boundaries, and stated expectations regarding payment of services. These interventions are to clients whose lives are a whirlwind of broken promises, taboo subjects, uncertainty, insecurity, inconsistency, and reactivity a refuge of attention, consistency, peace, and security.

Bare attention flows in opposition to a life guided by

streams of unconscious habit patterns and emotional reactivity. Bare attention awakens us to the stones we stumble over due to the blindness of confusion or ignorance. It shines a light into the shadows of confusion and ignorance and finds our frustrated desires and suppressed resentments. Bare attention identifies and pursues the single threads of the closely interwoven threads of our thoughts, feelings, and actions, which have over the years formulated the tapestry of our life story.

Bare attention is the clear and single-minded awareness of what actually happens to us and in us at each successive moment of perception. It is the forerunner of insight. It is a way of being that is counter to the general manner by which we briefly and fleetingly know or experience the events or people within our daily schedules. Bare attention trains the mind to be detached, open, silent, and alert within the framework of the present moment. It is an intention to suspend all judgments and interpretations, and to simply note and dismiss them if and when they do occur.

The task within bare attention is to simply acknowledge what occurs just as it occurs. It is a process of inviting one's self back into the present, of being mindful of the moment, with the realization that our minds have taken us into an imaginative realm of fantasy, recollections, or discursive thoughts. It is a means by which to acquaint our selves with an object before our minds alter its presence through conceptual paint overlaid with interpretations.

Bare attention is undertaken with an intention to undo our general ways of being in the world, it is an intention of simply noting and not thinking, not judging, not associating, not planning, not imagining, not wishing. It notes each occasion of experience as it arises, reaches its peak and then fades away. It is a sustained mindfulness of experience in its bare immediacy, carefully and precisely and persistently.

Bare attention awakens me to the relationship I have formed with this world through the untested foundations of beliefs, values, guiding principles, and morals. To attend to what formulated these foundations I have found seeds of misconstrued concepts built out of my childhood fears and fantasies. I have seen a blind faith to family customs, rituals, and cultures. I have come to understand how some of the holy of holy concepts within my "absolute truths" are unquestioned beliefs which perpetuate suffering.

As nature prevents the presence of two thoughts within the same moment, those who implement the practice of bare attention into their daily lives will find that mindfulness serves to lessen the turmoil of anxiety, restrains the drive within impulsivity, and acquaints them, as an observer, to the dynamics of their suffering. With this in mind, this healing journey requires that I invest in becoming acquainted with an intellectual and intuitive awareness of being a mindful presence with myself as I strive to be within the therapeutic relationship. It is my thought that bare attention to the tapestry of images, thoughts, and feelings that arise and fade throughout this process will guide me in my search for the wisdom, trust, strength, silence, and acceptance that are necessary for me to bring about a cessation of suffering.

A pumpkin placed on the surface of a pond soon
floats away and always remains on the water's

surface. But a stone does not float away; it stays where it is put and at once sinks into the water until it reaches bottom. Similarly, when mindfulness is strong, the mind stays with its object and penetrates its characteristics deeply. It does not wander and merely skim the surface as the mind destitute of mindfulness does.

~ Bhikkhu Bodhi

II

THE STILLNESS OF SILENCE

BEING STILL

Those with wings have no roots.
Those with roots cannot fly.

I awaken to the mourning dove's appeal for the sound of another, and find the passing dream state, like many before, was spent wandering through a petrified forest unlike any created by the ancient uniting of Gaea, Mother Earth, and Uranus, Father Heaven. It was filled with a longing, a seeking; it was a series of moments of futile endeavors.

As I walked upon moonlit pathways, edged by shadows of hidden yesterdays as well as shrouded by entangled memories, I encountered afterimages, echoes, phantoms, fragmented sequels, refrains, and vague specters. Now and then, it felt as though I had stepped on a "mind-trap" and suddenly became entangled inside an invisible emotional net that swirled me around and around from one apparition to another. Each apparition messaged that I have gone around and around in discursive circles once, twice, a thousand times throughout my lifetime of nights. I say to myself, "I've been here before. I've re-imaged, revisited, and reviewed past moments and choices as if I were an author rewriting a long ago discarded novel. I am displaced and lost." Within this uncertainty is a childhood mandate to settle down beside a stilled pool of water and wait. Wait for a teacher, a guide, a companion, a savior.

Saldage
Standing at the Threshold
With uncertainty, I question:
What is it that I seek?
Protection? Compassion? Acceptance? Forgiveness?
Completion?
Who is it that I beckon?
A father? A mother? A sister? A brother? A
companion? A child? A god?
To be? To endure? To offer? To embrace? To
validate?
An intentional presence that is drawn upon
A place and time of shadows, myths, and dreams?
Birthed within a family?
Matured within a relationship?
Nourished within a community?
Where the Stillness within Silence,
Affirms the exchange of life's giving and taking,
Embraces the connection of life's emotional threads,
and
Observes the interdependence of life with non-
judgmental awareness,
Yet, knows of a united oneness with another that
can not be?
Since it can not be, do I yearn
To know integration through the formation of
thought;

To see clarity through the flowing of ink; and
To feel completion through the act of creating?
And then, finally, within the stillness of silence,
I befriend
An internal companion with whom
There is an honoring of the who and what of which I
am;
A woman, a daughter, a sister, a niece, a wife, a
mother, an aunt, a grandmother.
I touch
With reverence the presence of all that was, is, and
will be.
I release
The seeking, the beckoning, the yearning to the
Winds of Change.
I with uncertainty, Step over the Threshold
Foreseeing the return.

In making things end and in making things start,
there is nothing more glorious than keeping still.

To sit, within stilled silence, mindful of the in-and-out flow of the breath begins the practice known as tranquility meditation. This is an intentional act of "calling into existence or producing" tranquility through mindfulness upon an identified object. Tranquility is a concentrated, unshaken, peaceful, and unsullied state of mind.

For some people meditation is shrouded in esoteric mystery. Others understand it through images of a person sitting in the lotus position with eyes half-closed. Others associate it with holiness and spirituality. In its most general sense it is deciding exactly how to focus the mind for a period of time and then doing just that.

In theory, focusing the mind upon an object sounds very easy, but practice acquaints us with a mind that seems to have a will of its own as it drifts from one thought, image, conversation, or memory to other remembrances, conversations, concepts, and thoughts. This internal stream goes on and on like a personal conversation with oneself or a perpetual story upon a movie screen. The more one attempts to pull in or control this wandering mind, the more it refuses to comply.

Therefore, at the point when one realizes that the mind has traveled here and there, one is simply to note this to oneself and with acceptance gently return again to the meditative object. Therefore, an important therapeutic value within one's meditation practice is the development of a nonjudgmental attitude about whatever arises, without picking and choosing, as well as the encouragement to develop unconditional compassion for the self. This practice of gently bringing self back introduces us what is known as the observing mind and over time allows us to develop a distinction between being in the flow of our thoughts and sensations and being aware of an observing "I."

Noting and labeling impulses, images, thoughts, and feelings messages a position that what arises is not "unnatural"; yet natural does not always mean beneficial. Therefore, meditation is an avenue by which to awaken us to and be conscious of our body, mind, feelings, and perceptions. It encourages an effective means by which to contain disturbing thoughts and feelings, similar to the containment of a campfire by fire ring stones, and thus increase one's ability to not be governed by detrimental thoughts and feelings. This is in opposition to attempts to extinguish suffering through coping skills such as projection, suppression and repression.

Meditation also acquaints us to the repetitive themes that impact the quality of our daily life and invites insight into impermanence, suffering, and non-self. The development of a practice that includes the extension of small increments of time has the potential to introduce to the student of meditation personal themes of anxiety, restlessness, and impulsivity, thus encouraging the development of skills such as self discipline, affect tolerance, and delay of gratification. Therefore, the cumulative benefit of meditation enhances mental and physical well-being as well as aids in the development of effective interpersonal dynamics.

Kaplan suggests that when one is in a meditative state, one has obtained the ability to turn off the faint after-images that are constantly with us and interfere with seeing objects with total clarity. He noted that when one is able "to turn off the spontaneous self-generated images . . . the beauty of the flower . . . seen in these higher states of awareness is indescribable [and] appears to radiate beauty."[5]

To understand the value of meditation one needs to go beyond the mere reading of it to discover the practice through an experiential acquaintance; that is, the truth of pudding can only be ascertained through the experience of eating pudding.

Hence it is a personal experience, a subjective experience, and consequently, each practitioner creates her own meditative style.

> *When the mind is restless it is not the proper time*
> *for cultivating the following factors of enlightenment:*
> *investigation of the doctrine, energy and rapture,*
> *because an agitated mind can hardly be quieted by*
> *them.*
> *When the mind is restless, it is the proper time for*
> *cultivating the following factors of enlightenment,*
> *tranquility, concentration and equanimity, because*
> *an agitated mind can easily be quieted by them.*
>
> ~ The Buddha

Feelings influence how we think, and our thoughts have an impact upon our feelings. Therefore, intense feelings disturb our thinking and thus increase suffering. When the mind is calm, our thoughts become clearer and we have greater freedom from tension and discontent. The presence of tension and discontent messages a need to regain control and restraint as well as suggests a need to

---

[5] Aryeah Kaplan, *Jewish Meditation: A Practical Guide* (New York, 1985), 9.

increase awareness and knowledge of one's motives. To undertake the practice of tranquility meditation is to develop a technique that settles and quiets mental activity. This form of quietness of mind is prescribed for those whose motivations are colored by craving.

Those whose lives are impacted by an unawareness of or an inability to see reality are encouraged to begin the practice of insight meditation. This is a method of mental analysis that acceptingly confronts every revealed motivation in the spirit of detached and objective contemplation. The task is to observe, to note, and to discern phenomena with utmost precision until their fundamental characteristics are brought to light. This process of analysis that encourages insight and the realization of wisdom is exercised in a more differentiated manner than tranquility meditation.

It is through bare attention upon an object that one achieves both serenity and insight. Serenity follows the primary chore of keeping the mind on the object and brings it back when one is aware that her thoughts have strayed away from the object and has wandered in random undirected thoughts. It also watches over the factors of the mind, catching the hindrances beneath their camouflages and expelling them before they cause harm.

> *The faculty of voluntarily bringing back a wandering attention, over and over again, is the very root of judgment, character, and will. No one is [master of himself] if he have it not. An education which should improve this faculty would be the education par excellence. But it is easier to define this ideal*

than to give practical instruction for brining it about.
~ William James

Students of meditation are encouraged to include an experienced teacher or a meditation partner in their practice. Also it is important to end each meditative practice with an activity that re-establishes one in objective reality prior to the return to daily activities; such as, dissolving of images, smelling incense or perfume, eating a light meal, naming each element in the environment, engaging in small talk with your meditation partner, or releasing the benefit obtained during a practice to all living beings.

An object of reflection used within meditation differs according to a person's temperament. At one time, qualified teachers identified which of forty objects would benefit a student's practice. These subjects include spherical images of various colors; the elements of fire, wind, space, light and water; decomposition of the body; mindfulness of the body; food; and the qualities of the Buddha. Everyone, regardless of their temperament, will benefit from a practice that includes a reflection upon the nature of beings such as the Buddha, Christ, Tara, or Mary Mother of Christ; meditation on loving-kindness; mindfulness of the body; or reflections on death.

It is important to keep in mind that meditation begins with a quietness that precedes calmness or tranquility. Therefore, if during a practice tension, irritability, or fatigue arises with an intensity that impedes a return to the object of focus, it is recommended that the practice be terminated and undertaken at another time. The meditation goal that one identifies will be reached gradually over time with consistent and repetitive practice. Two essential tools are patience and self-acceptance. It is recommended that the beginner should start her practice by focusing attention on some quiet, readily available, rhythmic process - her breath. Many meditation disciplines use the breath as a meditative object. The in and out rhythm of our breath is guided by the unconscious mind and mirrors our moods. To bring bare attention upon the flow of the breath is to intentionally form a link between the conscious and unconscious aspects of ourselves.

Breathing Meditation

Choose a time that you can commit to on a regular basis. A good practice is at least 10 minutes a day, year after year. Create a place that is comfortable and that provides a solitary atmosphere of privacy, calmness, and silence. Silence is the key factor.

While meditation postures include standing, sitting, reclining, and walking, the most suitable posture for breathing meditation is the seated posture. The ideal sitting posture is the "lotus" pattern, with the feet turned up and resting on the opposite thighs. If this posture is uncomfortable, then sit cross-legged on a cushion or on a chair with both feet placed firmly on the ground. The half cross-legged posture is the posture of sitting with one leg bent. Another posture is sitting with the two feet tucked underneath the body. You may find yourself more supported and grounded by placing cushions in such a way that that your hips are higher than your knees.

Make sure your back is straight but not strained and

rigid. Feel the crown of your head reaching up to the sky and at the same time feel your sitting bones reaching down to the center of the earth. The head should be held straight, tilted a slight angle downwards with the nose perpendicular to the navel.

The hands should be placed gently on the lap, the back of the right hand over the palm of the left.

The eyes can be closed softly, or left half-closed, whichever is more comfortable. Your eyes are seeing but not looking. Your jaw is relaxed. Place your tongue behind the upper teeth. Relax your shoulders.

Set your intention for doing the meditation.

Place your attention on the place where the incoming and outgoing breaths enter and leave the nostrils. This will be felt as a spot beneath the nostrils or on the upper lip, wherever the sensation of the air coming in and out of the nostrils can be felt most distinctly.

Breathe in mindfully; breathe out mindfully with well-placed mindfulness. The key to this practice is to be mindful of the spot where the in-breaths and the out-breaths are felt entering and leaving the nostrils and to maintain a steady and consistent awareness of the touch sensation of the breath.

Be with the beginning, the middle and the end of each in-breath and out-breath. The beginning of the in-breath is the start of the inhalation, the middle is continued inhalation, and the end is the completion of the inhalation. Likewise, in regard to the out breath, the beginning is the start of the exhalation, the middle is the continued exhalation, and the end is the completion of the exhalation.

If you attempt to trace the breath from the nose

through the chest to the belly, or to follow it out from the belly through the chest to the nose, your concentration will be disrupted and your mind will become agitated. Also, an attempt to control or hold back your breath with conscious effort will lead to fatigue and the interruption of mental concentration

As you note the sensation of your breath entering, begin to count the movement. The mere counting is not itself meditation, it is an essential aid to meditation. The easiest method of counting breaths is to count the first as "one, one"; the second as "two, two"; the third as "three, three"; the fourth as "four, four"; the fifth as "five, five" and so on up to the tenth breath which is counted as "ten, ten." Then return to "one, one" and continue again up to "ten, ten." This is repeated over and over from one to ten.

As you focus on the sensations of your breath, various thoughts and feelings will arise. You will become aware of how your mind jumps from one thought to another. Meditation is not a practice designed to repress or negate whatever may arise, so when you become aware of your wandering mind or arising feelings, be gentle and accepting with the simple acknowledgment of "thinking" or "feeling" and return your focus to your breath with the count of "one, one."

Close your mediation with a dedication of merit, dedicating any good that came during your practice to the benefit of others.

As you grow in your breathing meditation there is an awareness of and relationship with the ebb and flow of feelings and thoughts as they arise and fade. This is the beginning of insight into impermanence.

THE FIVE HINDRANCES

What may interfere with one's practice is the awakening of one of the five hindrances: restlessness and remorse, intention to experience desirable experiences, ill-will, indecisiveness and a divided heart, foggy-mindedness and apathy. These hindrances block our ability to move away from our investment in the self and to truly acknowledge the interdependence and interconnectedness of all living beings. They are intertwined into the suffering within, "the good I would do, I do not. The evil I would not do, I do."

Restlessness and remorse overpower our minds like wind stirs and agitates a pond, producing waves and ripples on the surface. Boredom and craving for desirable experiences create mental states equal to a pot of water that has been colored with red, yellow, blue, and orange dye. That is, when we are overpowered by desires and cravings, we are not able to foresee consequences and are not able to recall moral lessons learned long ago. Ill will is like a pot of water heated on the fire. The seething and boiling keeps us prisoner to aversion and hatred. Indecisiveness and a divided heart impacts our ability to reflect upon our feelings and behaviors as our minds are like a pot of water that is turbid, stirred up and muddy. Foggy-mindedness and apathy overcomes and takes us hostage as if we were being smothered by algae and water plants.[6]

Restlessness is known as the agitation that propels us

---

[6] Weragoda Sarada Ven Theor, *Treasury of Truth,* Buddha Dharma Education Association, 774-78; Nyanaponika Thera, *The Five Mental Hindrances and Their Conquest* (1993).

from one thought to another as thoughts swing from greed to aversion and from attachment to discontent. Worry comes from the remorse we have about past mistakes and the subsequent anxiety that follows imaged consequences. When agitation and remorse appears it is like trying to see one's reflection in a pond being swept by the wind.

To contain restlessness and worry one must first acknowledge its presence without being drawn into its current by noting, "restlessness and worry is rising within me." As they are abandoned, "restlessness and worry within me is abandoned." While they fade, "restlessness and worry is ceasing within me." When they are gone, "there is no restlessness and worry present within me."

Restlessness and worry are most effectively countered by turning the mind to a simple object that tends to calm it down; the method usually recommended is mindfulness of breathing, attention to the in-and-out flow of the breath.

The Art of Healing Sounds and Colors may also assist with the abandonment of worry and restlessness. This practice begins with two long in-breaths each followed by a cleansing out-breath sigh. On the third in-breath, imagine purified energy rising from the earth into your spleen followed by the release of toxic energy with the sound of *hoooo* as you exhale. After two complete visualizations, imagine your body absorbing the color yellow with your next in-breath. As you exhale release any remaining negative energy with the sound *hoooo* as you exhale.[7]

In stillness there is fullness,

---

[7] For more information about healing sounds, see Katzman and Shoshanna, *Qigong for Staying Young* (New York, 2003).

in fullness there is nothingness,
in nothingness there are all things.

~ Anonymous

SCORPIONS AND FROGS

As I sit quietly focused upon the in and out flow of the breath, my attention shifts to the sounds of children playing. I acknowledge the sounds and gently return to the breath. Then I find my attention has been drawn to a tightness between my shoulder blades. I note the physical sensation and return to the flow of the breath. I awaken inside a memory. I label this "remembering" and return to the breath. I find myself adjusting the monthly budget. I internally say, "worrying" and with acceptance return to the breath. Within the space where thoughts settle before arising again, I encounter what I identify as a fleeting moment of clarity. Then I come to an awareness that I have embarked upon yet another stream of consciousness, I label the awakening moment, "thinking, thinking", and return to the breath. For a passing second, I touch upon an idea of single-pointed tranquil absorption. It fades. I again return to the in-and-out flow of the breath. My vision clears and I comprehend a path free of attachment, aversion, and closed heartedness and mindedness. Rapture surprises me, and as it fades my mind undertakes a search to identify what were the preceding thoughts, images, techniques, and conditions that came together in such a manner that opened the door to this wonderful feeling. Desire intensifies into greed, which transforms into craving which stirs clinging. A greedy nature awakens an angry nature.

The still center of being . . . whispers, "Realize Me."
No sooner is it glimpsed then it is gone.

~ Guigo

A Fable

Once upon a time, a scorpion asked a frog to ferry him across a river. The frog replied that his fear of being stung by the scorpion prevented him from granting the request. The scorpion, in reply, eased the frog's anxieties with the notation that if he were to sting him then both of them would surely drown. With this seemingly safe guarantee, the frog agreed. About half way in their crossing, the scorpion stung the frog. As the frog was dying, he implored the scorpion to tell him why he doomed both of them to their deaths. The scorpion simply noted, "I'm a scorpion; it's my nature."

> *The mountain lake is fed*
> *not only by the outside rains,*
> *but also*
> *by springs welling up*
> *from within its own depths.*
>
> ~ Nyanaponika Thera

Within the mind is a storehouse of seeds that entered our psyche through the windows of our five senses: ears, nose, eyes, skin, and tongue. These vast and multiple seeds – images, memories, learned associations, concepts, ideas, and beliefs – lie latent in our mental storehouses like the slumbering Snow White, in wait for a particular trigger or condition. While it is a kiss from a prince that awakens Snow White, it is the fruit of past deeds that awakens a sleeping seed.

The transitory awakening of a memory, idea, or belief serves to close shades of varying degrees of transparency between us and the real world and sets us upon an internal journey from one thought or image to another. At times, there is a suppressed memory or an emotionally laden belief that, when triggered, emerges with such force that we are overtaken by rapid currents of mental confusion and emotional chaos and are thus lost to anxiety, irrationality, impulsivity, and delusions. These streams of consciousness move us through various feeling and mental states and may awaken other slumbering seeds.

These various states of "not seeing" arise from a defense mechanism that is drawn from the motivation to keep painful feelings and thoughts at bay; yet, the call to arms is drawn from a protective stance against the ghosts of yesterdays' battles. As we move throughout our days unaware of the present moment due to repetitive stimuli, habit patterns, or engagement with our mental stories, the impressions that bubble up are not of "this world" as they are the uniting of mind, imagination, and mind consciousness. They formulate the quality of our thoughts, our attitudes. The result is that the mental and behavioral responses to these transitory awakenings serve to plant additional seeds within the darkness of our unconscious.

These mental formations shape how we view the world; they give us a frame of reference and eventually through their repetitive appearance they formulate our intrinsic nature, our temperament. It is suggested that these habitual patterns that are ephemeral but are kammically potent can be classified into seven major categories: greed, hate, ignorance, faithful, intelligent, ruminating, and speculative. The combination of these natures (with the exception of speculative) with one another formulates 63 different types. The speculative type brings the total to 64 temperaments.

The majority of people will find that their temperaments include the variables of greed and hatred. There are others whose nature is ignorance and thus confusion and delusional thinking impact their lives. Akin to this nature are those whose minds oscillate; they are unable to focus their attention deliberately on one thing. Some people are exceptionally devoted, while others are exceptionally intelligent. Our personalities generally consist of a combination of 2 to 3 of these types. We can begin to acquaint ourselves with our primary nature through an exploration of our usual day-to-day behavior patterns, thoughts, and moods.

The greed temperament is derived from being attached to excitement, validation, power, and sensual experiences. This nature is defined by materialism, indulgence, acquisitiveness, covetousness, and selfishness. An acquisitive person craves to collect, hoard, and possess things. There is indulgence in sensuous pleasure absent of shame as well as subsequent guilt. She has a tendency to be wily, cunning, and proud. Her relationships are impacted by self-interest, entitlement, quarreling, and strife. This disposition is infectious as manifested within a commercialized, consumer-driven society.

The hateful nature is an angry person filled with self-centered pride, vengeance, wrath, spite, envy, jealousy, cruelty, and resentment. What other temperaments view as trivial will arouse anger within this nature. She is known to respond with violent reactions to unpleasant visual, auditory, scent experiences that include abusive words filled with hate and wrath. She and her loved ones suffer due to revenge, envy, jealousy, and prideful stubbornness. The disposition of this person is opposite to those of a devoted or an intelligent temperament.

The person with a faithful nature is one who finds refuge in her religious community, doctrine, and leaders. She is identified through her civilized, liberal, generous, devoted, gentle, and truthful behaviors.

The intelligent-natured person relies on reason and does not believe easily. She is seen as the opposite of hateful, as she is free from envy and resentment. She is not reactive or impulsive as her actions are drawn from mindfulness and wisdom and her fondness for virtuous deeds. She is a willing student when she views her teachers as wise.

The nature of ignorance is derived from dullness, forgetfulness, inattentiveness, and/or laziness. Her life is impacted by confusion and absence of motivation to think things through. She is seen as lazy, indolent, apathetic, and bored. Within relationships she follows the opinions of others and often suffers unnecessarily when led by those absent of wisdom and moral guidelines.

The ruminating-natured person thinks things over and throughout without accomplishing much. She oscillates and remains stuck within uncertainty and skepticism. Her life is impacted by her tendency to endlessly ponder and talk and not implement a plan of action.

The speculative natured person is one who merely rationalizes existing preferences and prejudices; therefore, her logic is absent of imagination.

Happiness lies not in the ability
to satisfy our every desire,
but rather in the ability
to refrain from reacting compulsively
to every craving and prodding of the mind.

~ Peter Ontl

Purifying Meditation

Sit in a comfortable position and allow your shoulders to relax. Keep your back straight as your spine supports your body. Quietly allow your body and mind to settle into the moment by bringing your awareness to the rhythm of your breath. As tranquility settles your mind, visualize a person who personifies compassionate wisdom. This person may be the Buddha, Christ, Tara, Mary Mother of Christ, or a Native American healer. As your mind's eye envisions this person you feel the image's tranquil, peaceful, and loving presence.

From the crown of this image's head a white radiating light rises up and enters your body through the top of your head. This white light is composed of the nature of blissful energy and as it enters your body it purifies the toxins within your body and renews the functioning of your entire nervous system.

A red light radiates from the compassionate being's throat and enters your vocal center with the sensation of bliss. As this sensation pervades your speech center all negative talk is purified and divine qualities of speech are awakened.

Then, from the image's heart, infinite radiant blue light comes to embrace your heart, purifying your mind of all its detrimental conceptions. Your ego, as well as the ignorance that feeds your greed and ill-will, are all purified in this blissful, blue radiance. Your indecisive mind which is held prisoner by internal conflict and doubt is clarified. Also purified is the closed heart and mind that is unable to see reality because its narrow perspective blocks new understanding. As the light enters your mind, your heart becomes like the blue sky, embracing universal reality and all of space.

The warmth, compassion, and wisdom of this image is permeating every cell of your body. You feel positive changes within your heart, mind, and body and wish to share this bliss with others. Imagine yourself going through the routine of your day in which you re-engage this clarity through mindfulness and as a result positively impact the relationship you have with family, neighbors, coworkers, and friends. Then visualize this newfound compassion being tested in some way and for a few moments you feel derailed from your positive intentions. Observe your self acknowledging these feelings, thoughts, and behaviors with compassion and regaining the radiance of loving-kindness and equanimity.

Allow the image to fade as you shift your focus upon the in and out rhythm of your breath. Allow the sounds in the room to come to you and greet the sounds that flow into the room from outside. Open your eyes and look about room identifying the objects in the room. Feel the joy that arises with a half-smile and dedicate the benefit of this exercise to the first person who comes to mind.

The appearance in the mind of undesirable and ignoble
thoughts, even if they are fleeting and only half-
articulate, has an unplesant effect upon one's self-
esteem.

~ Nyanaponika Thera

III

THE JOURNEY OF *SALDAGE*

THE PETRIFIED FOREST

May I find the Wisdom that silences the fortress of my mind's discontent so I may hear with understanding teachings absent of greed, anger, and ignorance.

I often feel as though I am an old blind woman walking through a petrified forest with only a staff to ensure that my steps find solid ground. I remain ignorant, as I unconsciously look away from that which will break my heart and seek stability through the creation of and attachment to ideas, beliefs, principles, and concepts. I yearn for certainty; anger erupts each time I stumble and fall and forges a dogmatic fortress that encircles my heart and mind. The desire to hear with understanding teachings absent of greed, anger, and ignorance speaks of an awareness of how this protective barrier deafens me to words of wisdom that shed light into the shrouded mysteries of life. During those moments when I find myself attempting to engage the unknown, I ask of myself, "What energies would flow into a life emptied of greed, anger, and ignorance?"

As I reflect upon the fortress of my mind's discontent,

an imagined stained and scratched door opens before me as if to invite me into a dark and musty attic. As my eyes scan beyond the entrance, I see streaks of yellowed sun beams, weakened by dust laden drapes; a scuffed wooden floor, covered by a bare-thread carpet of muted colors; and wall paper, grayed and yellowed, tugged away at the top most of a corner by the collected weight of long ago wisps of cigarette smoke.

My observing mind notices that there is no other furniture other than two rocking chairs placed facing each other in the center of the room. Sitting in one is a slender child. She seems to be no older than four years old. A slight musty scent of aged vanilla greets me as I enter the room with a request that the child not be disturbed. The sound of her voice, which I first heard as a distant mumble, intensifies into an animated stream of words. The words seem to rush from her with such passion that a focused listener would surrender to an impulse to talk over the justifying, rationalizing, point—counter-point, argumentative, single-person monologue.

I stand quietly at the edge of the room listening not to the words but to the power within her words and note to myself, "Her words are gushing out from a center of guilt, shame, remorse."

I again return to her words and listen so deeply that a crinkle forms on my forehead as I wonder, "Is there anxiety about a deed so wrong it is punishable by banishment?"

I quiet my distracting thoughts and listen even more

deeply and then I acknowledge a profound sadness in the threads of defensive anger that is begging to be heard and understood.

My observing mind becomes silent as my speculative nature begins to question if the cause of her profound sadness is within the Tibetan Wheel of Suffering. This Wheel illustrates how our psychological patterns – our unconscious drives and needs, impulsive and reactive responses, learned and conditioned habits, and obsessions and compulsions – serve to keep us locked in self-defeating or misguided mental formations.

The Tibetan Wheel of Suffering

Within this hub, the center point of our suffering, are the three united poisons of the mind: ignorance, hatred, and greed, symbolized, respectively, by a black pig chasing a red rooster chasing a green snake chasing a black pig.

To lessen the anxiety inherent in a world of uncertainty and ongoing change, our minds create fabrics of consistency as they intertwine the threads of past experience with those of inference of a yet to be experienced future. Thus, we interact with the world through conceptual lenses that color reality in various shades of truth. The black pig demonstrates the ignorance that arises when our minds defend against the anxiety of impermanence and powerlessness and our hearts are shielded from the suffering within grief and loss.

These barriers tell us that the inability of the energy within our anger and aversion to satisfy, ensure, or retain our endless desires have been redirected inward, and thus we are paralyzed by confusion, delusions, and/or depression. Within this state of closed-mindedness and closed-heartedness we find that our life energy is drained and thus we encounter fatigue, forgetfulness, inattentiveness, worthlessness, helplessness, boredom, and mistrust.

The confusion illustrated by the pig also tells us of the suffering within the relationship dance of approach-avoidance due to yearning for physical and emotional closeness, while fearing the loss of self through unrestrained emotional fusion. The blackness of the pig tells us how ignorance blinds and deafens us to the wisdom that accompanies compassion, loving-kindness, sympathetic joy, and equanimity. The true antidote to ignorance is understanding.

From this fundamental blindness and deafness is born the rooster and the snake. The rooster symbolizes how excessive desire leads to the greed within: "I wish, I want, I must have, and I will have." Our desires are manifested in our passion to possess objects and/or people, through our attachments to beliefs and ideas, and in our subtle clinging to spiritual experiences. The color red tells how greed is like a flame, hot and restless, and keeps the cool peace of non-attachment at bay.

Due to the anxiety that arises with imperfection, impermanence, and interdependency, we are forever "clinging" to things, each other, and ourselves in a mistaken effort to obtain and control that which we believe will ensure security. The emptiness illustrated by the rooster also tells us of the suffering trapped within the relational dance of avoidance-approach, escaping internal meaningless while yearning for physical and emotional closeness. When ignorance intertwines with attachment, one's relationship with people will be colored by pretentiousness, deceit, shamelessness, inconsideration, heedlessness, and distraction.

As one reflects upon the excesses of greed, one soon becomes acquainted with the force of insatiable emptiness that energizes frustration, disappointment, confusion, aversion, and hatred. Greed also brings forth meanness, inflated self-esteem, mental dullness, agitation, surprise, and hidden intentions. The true antidote of greed is contentment.

The green snake portrays the anger and aversions that arise when we do not get what we want, when we get what we do not want, or we lose what we want. This snake is manifested through our emotional, mental, and physical distancing patterns; postures of assertiveness; hostile thoughts; untruthful, malicious or angry words; and physical aggression. It arises as wrath, resentment, spite, envy, jealousy, and cruelty.

Therefore, it is hatred and aversion that feeds separation, marginalization, alienation, and interpersonal distress. Aversion also speaks of reactivity that comes from a fear of contamination. Hatred tells us of a covert clinging to unmet desires. The anger illustrated by the snake also tells us of the suffering within being trapped within the human dance of avoidance-avoidance due to a rejection a physical and emotional closeness that is driven by the evasion of the emptiness within self. The greenness of the snake indicates how anger and aversion poisons and strangles compassion, sympathetic joy, and equanimity. The true antidote of hatred is loving-kindness.

Thus, these three symbols depicted in the center hub, spinning around, endlessly, each having in its mouth the tail of the image in front, show that these states are inseparably connected within our hearts and minds. The arousal of one tells us that the other two are lurking somewhere in the shadows of our hearts and minds.

Various Tibetan paintings of the Wheel of Suffering place three images upon a blue background. The background tells us that while our thoughts are often symbolized as a monkey jumping from one tree branch to another, as a flame moving from one candlewick to another, as leaves floating upon a steam, or as moving clouds, the true nature of mind is as vast and pure as a cloudless blue sky. Therefore, while craving, anger, and ignorance are powerful they are, in themselves, void of any permanent and true substance.

Around the center hub is the first ring, one half of the circle having a white background and the other half black. Three individuals are ascending in the white half of the circle to the upper three realms of existence: the realm of asuras, of devas, and of humans. This is the path of good conduct in mind, speech, and body that people undertake as they move from the light to light or to the light from darkness.

These images confirm the sense of well-being that comes from a life that is lived in congruence with one's morals, guiding principles, and beliefs. They show how right view sharpens and redefines one's cognitive faculties whether it be sensory cognition, thinking, memory, imagination, or insight knowledge. They also validate the movement towards recovery that occurs after a person acknowledges how her drug/alcohol use has resulted in the violation of personal moral boundaries. Often, it is within this time of blackness that a person's thinking will shift from the stage of pre-contemplation, "I don't have a problem" to contemplation, "Maybe I do have a problem."

Within the realm of asura are beings whose quarrelsome nature resulted in their fall from the heavens and who now enviously try to invade the celestial realms. They are unaware of the aggressive nature of their jealousy and envy. They also are blind to the pain they create as they approach, destroy, and assimilate obstacles that come between them and their entitlements. The anger and resentment within their covetousness hampers the timing, mastery, self control, and adaptation necessary to effectively manage frustrations, change situations, and encounter new experiences.

Included within each of the six realms is a tiny figure symbolizing a bodhisattva. These spiritual warriors are compassionate beings whose sole and unique purpose in this world is to work for the benefit of all beings. Inserted in the asura realm is a bodhisattva wielding a flaming sword, representative of discriminating awareness needed to free one paralyzed by their own aggression.

The beings within the upper regions of the deva realm are those who experience meditative rapture, serene joy, or sublime equanimity. They are those who give themselves over to peak experiences in their desire for the temporarily dissolution of physical, emotional, and mental separateness. The craving for a sense of "at-oneness" with significant others results in a suffering that comes either as a fear of the isolation that comes with separation or a fear of absorption that arises with togetherness. They experience the suffering that arises through the impermanent and insubstantiality of pride.

Within in this realm is a bodhisattva holding a lute signifying the joy and happiness that arises from a peaceful mind in unison with sensory experience. The sound of the lute also alerts those in this realm that pleasures are temporary and that the happiness that comes with letting go of the emotional fusion with self and with another far exceeds that which arises from indulgence.

The human realm contains beings whose suffering arises from the human life cycle: birth, illness, and death. They grasp at a consistent and permanent self and fiercely defend against a sense of insubstantiality. Their suffering arises as they cling to people, objects, ideas that validate desired images of self and as they reject anything that threatens or invalidates their imagined identity. Their suffering is found within vague and disturbing feelings of insecurity, aloneness, emptiness, falseness, and alienation.

Placed within the human realm is a bodhisattva holding an alms bowl and staff symbolizing an ascetic engaged in a true comprehension of identity.

Within the black half of the circle, there are three images descending from light into darkness or from darkness into darkness. They depict how the driving energy of anxiety draws beings through various degrees of neurosis or psychosis. Sometimes these images are shown as being chained together and pulled downward by a demoness, Tanha, into one of the three lower realms of existence: the realm of the hungry ghost, of hell, and of animals.

Those within the animal realm are beings whose lives are defined by their love of self-indulgence and attachment to sensory pleasures. They are the hunted and the hunter and some are characterized by stupidity and servitude. Due to the fleeting nature of all experiences, these beings find themselves endlessly returning to states of impoverishment, unrest, separation, desire, or tension. They are blind to the negative consequences that are fed by their impulsivity and delusions. Their distraction hinders the development of peace, harmony, and interdependence with others.

Included in this realm is a bodhisattva holding a book representing the need for wisdom that arises through thought, speech, and reflection.

Hell is the lowest and worst of the three lower realms where beings are perpetually swinging between states of frozen frigidness and tormenting heat. They are suffering from an assortment of internal and hideous punishments; they are wracked by their own anger, fear, paranoia, aggression, and anxiety. Their suppression, repression, and rejection of unwanted feelings as well as resentful and self-righteous attitudes keep them forever riveted to their self-scripted movie scenes.

Shown in this realm is a bodhisattva holding a mirror indicating that the seeing and acknowledging, with nonjudgmental awareness, of unwanted emotions will alleviate their suffering.

The realm of the hungry ghost is filled with beings with long, extremely slender necks, needle mouths, and bloated stomachs. They are characterized by their infinite emptiness and eternal starvation that drives addictive and compulsive behaviors. When they do obtain what they crave, their achieved desires turn into swords and knives in their bellies. Their unfulfilled longings and cravings torture them through unending grief, rejection, bargaining, and anger. They remain insatiably obsessed with the fantasy of achieving complete release from their past. Their efforts to undo the past remain unproductive as they layer past memories onto the present and thus respond to present occurrences as if they were suddenly transported into their past. While they are aware of the suffering within their misery, they are unaware of how their confusion and delusion comes from their transpositions and subsequent mistaken attributions.

Introduced in this realm is a bodhisattva holding a bowl filled with spiritual nourishment. These spiritual morsels: grace, faith, mindfulness, centeredness, compassion, loving-kindness, and equanimity, all contain the nutrients of wisdom to ease their torments.

Completing the Wheel is the image of death embracing the outermost circle of twelve linking images of dependent origination. These images illustrate the rebirth of suffering within the time frames of the present, future, and past. In any given situation there are seeds that will give rise to the next situation, therefore the simple happening of a state is dependent on its antecedent state. A state arising is simultaneously fading.

If one comes across a person who has been shot by an
arrow, one does not spend time wondering about

where the arrow came from, or the caste of the
individual who shot it, or analyzing what type of
wood the shaft is made of, or the manner in which
the arrowhead was fashioned. Rather, one should
focus on immediately pulling out the arrow.

~ The Buddha

My compassionate self moves to the young child. As she embraces the young child, she begins to rock and whisper, gently, softly, "How long have you been here?" The young child tells of wakening to this room after a night of hiding under blankets trying to be unseen, holding her breath trying to be unheard, swallowing her fear trying to be still as the sounds of distant shattering glass and disembodied voices crashed and stumbled upon and into each other.

My compassionate self hears of the homesickness that emerged with such intensity that it overflowed her soul and traveled across rivers, over mountains, and through valleys searching for someone to bring her home. The yearning returned from its fruitless travels and surrounded her as if it were the voice of an unseen other. In a painfully frustrated response, anger roused within the child an intention to destroy this other's yearning that come in the place of her heart's desire.

My compassionate self awakens to the realization that this young child is ignorant of the fact that the chair opposite her is empty and that she is being persecuted by a phantom of her own creation. Slowly my compassionate self understands how this young child's powerlessness created not a monologue but an internal dialogue between a phantom, lost within her homesickness, and a child, lost within her wounds. My mind recalls the story of Narcissus who believed that the image in his reflection was a water spirit with the same characteristics as Apollo, and hears how this child's unproductive attempts to be heard and understood by her own echo has condemned her to remain forever alone in this shadowy dust-filled room. Narcissus clung to the image of his love; she clings to the sound of her anger.

Touching the present moment, we come to know the past created the present and together the future is being created.

"*Shu-shu*", my compassionate self whispers as she rocks the small child with the sound of ancient mother's loving-kindness. "*Shu-shu*, feel the sadness within you, hear its voice, be with it's tone and texture, and release this caged discontent with the outward flow of my breath. *Shu-shu*. Silence your thoughts and listen only for the sounds within this room." And together, they rocked back and forth, listening to the sounds in the room.

My compassionate self moves to the empty chair opposite the small child. I begin the practice of 'Giving and Taking'[8] by first resting my

---

[8] Tonglen meditation is a sitting practice that begins with breathing in the suffering of another and with the out-breath releasing to the other that which

thoughts and opening myself to silence. I then imagine a small black cloud filled with the child's aloneness, anger, sadness, and anxiety surround her heart. I feel the inky dark cloud move away from her heart and leave her body as it rides upon the gentle wind of my in-breath. It enters my body; it touches my heart, and a sudden sensation of wondrous energy spreads throughout my body.

A tiny silvery whisper emerges, "It is your wish to be released from this room so that you may walk with the summer sun and feel its warmth touch your face. You wish to see the multiple colored leaves blanket the sidewalk and hear them crackle as their scent is released into the autumn air. You wish to feel the tingle of the first winter's snow upon your tongue. You wish to release all that is frozen as the spring wind awakens mother earth. You wish to look into the eyes of others and see the reflection of love."

On my exhalation, I release to her those wishes on a white cloud knowing they will give her the courage to leave this room, to open her door to life.

Silently, the sun's rays departed to the west and unveiled the moon's spherical disk. A pause fills the room with stilled silence as if time paused to honor this universal transition. My compassionate self inquires, "Where in this moment is the voice of your phantom? How will you allow yourself to hear the emptiness within this room and then know the other chair holds no one? What will you do with this absence? When will you give yourself permission to greet this absence, acquaint yourself with it, feel it, know it

---

will ease their suffering. This flow of talking and giving is similar to the therapeutic art of unconditional positive regard and empathetic and reflective listening.

in its entirety, and allow it to settle within? I wonder what will open your mind to see that what your words attempt to harm, silence, or destroy is but a memory and thus you are in a perpetual state of cyclical suffering.

"Your desire to be heard and understood can be heard and understood only by you, not this phantom of a memory. I appeal to your imaginative skills to see and hear how you, as this phantom and small child, wish to be free from suffering, wish to be happy.

"Each time you become aware that you once again have entered this room and are engaged in a confrontation with your phantom, trust in the freedom that accompanies the awareness that both you and this transitory memory wish to be free from suffering. Breathe in with your whole body an image of your phantom's pain; on your out breath release to your memory the happiness, joy, and calmness of mind that will bring an end to it's suffering. This practice of 'Giving and Taking' is the silver key that opens a door to a space of tranquil abiding."

The Buddha suggested that whatever it is that we reflect upon frequently becomes the inclination of our mind. If one recurrently thinks greedy, hostile, or harmful thoughts, desire, ill will, and harmfulness shape the mind. If one repeatedly thinks in the opposite way, compassion, loving-kindness, sympathetic joy, and equanimity become the preference of the mind. The direction we take always comes back to ourselves, to the intentions we generate moment by moment in the course of our lives.

Develop a Mind that Clings to Nothing

Embracing positive. Push out detrimental thoughts through the remembrance of small acts of compassion, kindness, and validation.

Reflecting pain. Negate delusive thoughts through the reflection of past consequences and the securitization of the harm that accompanies blame, self deceit, minimization, justification, rationalization, resentment, and entitlement.

Shifting attention. Refuse to give any attention to discursive ramblings as if they were horrid sights by shifting focus to external objects or contemplation of body or feelings.

Letting go. Relax painful thoughts through the mindful attention upon subtle muscular movements within the act of standing, walking, sitting, reading, talking, eating.

Tucking away. Carefully store detrimental thoughts in an imagined secure container.

Pushing away. Clamp down on self with forceful discipline through the clenching of teeth, pressing of the tongue on the roof of the mouth, crushing down the thoughts with a new awareness and intent until the thoughts are abandoned and subside.

The thought manifests as the word;
The word manifests as the deed;
The deed develops into habit;
And habit hardens into character;
So watch the thought and its ways with care,
And let it spring from love
Born out of concern for all beings .
As the shadow follows the body,
As we think, so we become.

As we think, so we become.

~ The Buddha

May I find the Loving Compassion that will soften
the shield embracing my heart so that I may love
absent of greed, anger, and ignorance.

I find myself standing on a dry dirt road with two deep parallel ruts cutting winding dark ribbons into the road until they unite and disappear in the horizon. The sun greets me with the same dry warmth that soothingly penetrates my skin as I wrap around me a towel just pulled from a tumbling clothes dryer. The air messages that it is a time of transition and I see the slight touch of autumn's mustard yellows and crimson reds upon the tips of trees lining a distant hill. Before me stands a child of about twelve years of age. Her head is bent down with absorbed attention upon the small puffs of dust clouds her bare feet stirs up before her.

She looks up at me with expectant eyes that suddenly overfill with tears. "I don't remember who or what I'm looking for," she says, as miniature rivulets begin to flow down her cheek.

Then I notice a three-year-old boy with wispy blonde hair and mesmerizing oxen-eyes as he emerges from his hiding place behind the girl. As he takes hold of her right index finger, he reaches up with his left hand and touches a teardrop that is forming along the girl's chin, asking "Find mummy?"

Suddenly, as if a whirlwind came down from the heavens in response to the boy's voice, I come to myself standing in the center of a frozen lake. I am shivering and see nothing more than a dark and shadowy forest surrounding me. I hear in the distance the sound of children's voices repeating a refrain with a haunting tone, "Broken hearts, frozen hearts, shattered hearts." And then I see them: four—no, five. Five hungry, child-like, ghosts with needle mouths, long twisted thin necks, and bloated stomachs.

They come out of the forest and stand along the lake's shoreline, repeating their refrain, "Broken hearts, frozen hearts, shattered hearts." Their words travel across the surface of the frozen lake and encircle me with the sounds of unfilled longings and infinite emptiness.

Then I awaken to my own craving for those who have been lost to me, those who have died. Within the darkness of this forest memories of past days rise and intermingle to become a swirling chaos within the image of emptiness where there once was a home, a family. Confusion, anger, and loneliness flash within as these memories incite feelings and memories that pummel upon me, one frozen memory after another.

I hear questions from a child. Confused, they come as fragments: "His heart was broken? Why did I have to go? They moved?" The sound of adolescent angst intertwined with arrogance swirls around me, as the questions become assertions: "I won't be here if he comes back! I'll do as I please." The mist in the air surrounds me with the chilling voice of others, accusing: "If you had faith, she could hear. You were her companion. It is you that must leave. It does not matter, it is over. I cannot help you." Then, "There was an accident." I feel myself falling upon the ice as I have fallen before with broken promises, beliefs, and dreams shattered all around me. I feel the layers of iced grief, anger, sadness, confusion shielding my heart. Again, the refrain, "Broken hearts, frozen hearts, shattered hearts."

The night cloud's fingertips drift away from the moon. In the silvery light I see visions of a small child, alone in the gray-toned shadows, planting seeds in the moist soil of despair. Her sob-filled voice fills the night's emptiness, "You are too stupid to understand. I don't need you. I'm special. I'll hide my tears. I won't tell you anything. I won't need you. I'll show you that I don't need you."

A veil lifts and my observing mind sees a raging powerless ego annihilating self-in-relationship, suppressing feelings; and all the while, unknowingly creating her shadowy forest of worthlessness, hopelessness, alienation, and pseudo-independence.

Wisdom tells me that I am nothing;
love tells me I am everything.
Between the two, my life flows.

I feel a golden-toned voice, vibrating the soft and gentle touch of loving-kindness. "These hungry ghosts are visions that arise from years of tears closeted within your soul. Is it now time to cut this intertwining craving and clinging to your yesterdays?" She encourages a thought that to be freed from this frozen place and time begins with a true comprehension of the refrain, "Broken hearts, frozen hearts, shattered hearts."

This voice says, "Call forth these five hungry ghosts, one by one, by their true given names and see each true 'I'-in-self hidden behind veils of greed, anger, and ignorance. Ask what it is that will cease their yearning and release them from this frozen forest so that they may finally rest in peace. As you hear their request touch your heart, open yourself to share with each that which will release you from this bondage. Melt this chain with loving-kindness and forge the golden key that gives admission to a room of healing serenity."

In a clearing I find myself slowly warmed by the autumn sun as I return to the two children I met earlier on a dry, dusty road. Behind me is the forest I have just emerged from; before me is a field of yellowed wheat. Just beyond the field is a house weathered gray by the seasons and weakened by the stresses of time. In the golden rays of the morning light, the young girl is kicking up clouds, searching through the barren soil for seeds of her past, and desiring to be freed from yesterday's delusions. She walks over to the side of the road and bends over; as she stands, I see three keys, dangling from her left hand. One key is silver, another is gold, and the third is made of diamonds. I feel the pain of fear awaken as the warmth of this early autumn day touches the frozen shield that embraces her heart.

The air is filled with sounds of a new refrain, "May I be happy. May I be free from pain. May I feel emotionally connected with others. May I be at peace.

"May these children be happy. May they be freed from pain. May they feel emotionally connected with others. May they be at peace.

"May those hungry ghosts be happy. May they be freed from pain. May they feel emotionally connected with others. May they be at peace."

Metta Meditation

The goal of meditation of loving-kindness is to wish happiness for all beings. This practice begins with first extending love to one's self by saying, "I will rid my mind of anger, hatred, ignorance, fear, greed, and craving. I will make my mind clear, fresh and pure. Like a transparent window is my mind and I pour out thoughts of love and kindness to myself."

The practice moves you to another as you recall a mental image of someone dear to you. Imagine yourself within their being, feel his or her personality, enter your own being and direct loving-kindness into the mind and heart of that person. Repeat this with other people with whom you feel emotionally close. In time extend this warmth and kindness to others in your life; for example, people who live in your neighborhood, the grocery clerk, your co-workers, and eventually all beings on earth and beyond.

If you find during this practice that disturbing thoughts and feelings arise in conjunction with an image of a person, take this as a message that it is not the right time to extend loving-kindness to this particular person. With self acceptance, return to extending warmth and loving-kindness to your self.

The arising of ill will hinders one's meditation practice. Ill will is a synonym for aversion. It is felt as hatred, envy, anger, self-pity, and resentment. It is seen in the repulsion we have towards others, objects, situations, and ourselves. An introspective mind that is overcome with ill will can be equated to a person looking for her reflection in a pot of boiling water.

To become mindful of ill will one must first discern it arising without acceptance of its justifications with, "ill will is rising within me." As it is abandoned, "ill will within me is abandoned." While it is fading, "ill will is ceasing within me." When it is gone, "there is no ill will present within me." To ease anger and ill will, one is directed to meditate on loving-kindness.

The Art of Healing Sounds and Colors may also assist with the abandonment of ill will. This practice begins with two long breaths each followed by a long sigh. With your third in-breath, imagine purified energy rising from the earth into your liver. Release toxic energy with the sound *shuuuu* with your out-breath. After you have completed three complete visualizations, imagine your body absorbing the color green with your next in-breath. As you exhale, release any remaining negative energy with the sound *shuuuu*.

May I find the Courage to withstand the crumbling
of my
delusions so that the light of right understanding
guides me on a life path absent of greed,
anger, and ignorance.

"To find a pathway absent of greed, anger, and ignorance" messages hope that there is indeed a way of life that leads out of this petrified forest in which there looms gigantic trees twisted and bent by an ego intent on creating a self-referenced world. Each tree has been tagged with a label that takes possession of it through the identification of "my memory", "my feelings", "my ideas", or "my dreams". Circling the trees are multiple pathways carved out by the anger of unmet desires and covered over by entangled vines driven by a need to satiate an unquenchable thirst. For years I have wandered in the shadows of this forest unable to see that it is of my own creation.

I come to a place where I envision myself eagerly standing before bookshelves, my eyes lightly and briefly touching upon one book's title and then another, feeling their words tickle my thoughts until I surrender to their unspoken promises. Once engaged by the promising nature of a title, it is hope that opens a book jacket and begins another journey through pages. With the turning of each page, desire seeks the experience of validation within the configuration of a writer's text. All of this, I believe, is driven by memory traces of how the words of unknown authors enfolded my emotional self as they alleviated the subsequent emotional chaos that followed the death of my father when I was three years old.

Later, literature provided me with alternate threads by which to darn a harmonious, yet delusional, understanding of death, of fatherless children, of a family. To move into this realm is to be cuddled in the arms of a chair, mesmerized by the pages of a book unfolding like an accordion, embraced by a transparent sound barrier, and transported into fantasies found through fictional characters. While my mind's eye grasped the hand of my naïve emotional self and together we observed the telling of storied lives, there was a seeking mind that simultaneously identified revealing markers to create a map, not to a place of hidden treasures, but to a place that felt like a home.

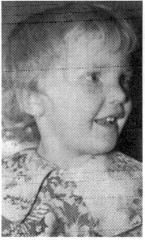

I was six years old the first time this happened. Martin and Cooney's *Five Little Peppers and How they Grew* eased my aloneness with the emptiness left by my father's death and filled it with a reformulated concept of family. Later, it was Alcott's characters within *Little Women* and *Little Men* who gave me permission to vicariously be a fatherless child united with loving adults who validated sacrifice, patience, and compassion. Burnett's themes of grief and loss within

The Little Princess identified the behaviors, choices, and attitudes necessary to survive the evils of dark despair until the rescue by an unknown and unidentified savior, just and righteous.

Around my twelfth year, I was introduced to the distinctive sounds within words like Cimarron, Shangri-La and Katmandu. Their syllables took possession of my young imagination and swept me away to exotic lands of my own creation, filled with visions of magical wonder and embracing atmospheres of peace and love. Through an innocent process of repeated readings with a "bias towards a notion pondered over," my suffering intertwined naïve beliefs into guiding principles and moral guidelines.

My memory recalls an incident in which I understood my mother to say that if I were to eat apple seeds they would collect in my appendix; as a consequence, I would die. From her stern warning, apple orchards were redefined as cemeteries reserved for naughty children. As an adult, I find humor in the manner by which my childhood mind intertwined apples with punishment, exclusion, and death especially in comparison with the Biblical story of Adam and Eve. Yet, there is a mysterious quality within myths that, despite the suffering they perpetuate, seem to become more precious than life.

Closed minds and hearts are the result of a failure of trust.

In response to a slight tugging at my shirtsleeve, my attention is redirected away from this search for answers within the words of others and into the eyes of a three-year-old child, who asks, "Find daddy?"

As my reflective mind enters the memories of this child self, the words of Padmasiridi De Silva come to mind: "Death of a loved one disturbs the relationships that sustain a person's sense of 'identity' and the high level of binding and cathexis concentrated on the person who is lost is suddenly disrupted . . . there is a close link between the doctrines of egolessness and suffering." Through this lens of Buddhist thought, I begin to feel a crumbling of a child's self with an understanding of how my father's absolute and final absence from our lives disrupted the multiple relationships between my father, mother, sister, and me.

Besides the sudden severing of the identity I was forming via my father, the connecting emotional threads between those of us that were left, although still intact, were unknowingly stretched and pulled by our own individual fears of egolessness.

My father's death left my mother, a young woman deaf from infancy, with two daughters and pregnant with her first son. I do not recall whose idea it was to wander outside the house early that morning as my mother slept. I can, however, imagine my young self following my older sister as if an invisible thread that tied us together tugged me along as she, with her five-year-old world view, undertook an emotional duty to find our father. Did we believe we could find him fly fishing in the creek that ran alongside the house? Or was there something about

71

the water that enticed us into abandoning our search? I can recall to this day the cessation of anxiety and arising rapture that coincided with my surrender to the inevitable. Two young men, I am told, rescued us both from this search for our father.

Shortly after this incident my mother remarried, and by the time I was seven years old, she was divorced and pregnant with her fifth child. Her fourth child, taken by his father in the dark of night, vanished within the tangled web of adults who regressed into childlike behaviors under incompetent custody laws.

My reflective mind recalls the unbound inquisitiveness that carried my six-year-old emotional self into the house from school knowing on that day my mother's fifth child was to be born. I can still feel the internal rebound that coincides with walking into an unseen plate of glass as my being absorbed, not the tone of grief, but the intensity of frustration within my grandmother's assertion, "The baby died!"

The Buddha's recommendation to abstain from false speech is found in the position that people connect with one another within an atmosphere of mutual trust, where each draws upon the belief that the other will speak the truth. It is suggested therefore that families and societies will fall into chaos as one untruth shatters trust, as it is the nature of lies to proliferate through attempts to weave a harmonious tapestry of reality.

When I reflect upon those times in which I experience an intense urge to say other than what I believe is true, I know it is fed by the anxiety intrinsic to uncertainty, and inherent with the aloneness of expulsion. At other times, the drive seems to come from a sense of nothingness that seeks validation through inclusion with others or continuity within mangled and haphazard memories. It feels as though it is an act that preserves or ensures a sense of control, power, or protection.

What this force blinds me to is the powerlessness that coincides with the telling of an untruth, as well as the emotional separation that overlaps the fear of discovery. It also creates the need for another story to support the one prior. Therefore, the beliefs that compel me to lie are but a layer of lies within a lie.

The intensity of my grandmother's words served to erect an unbreakable barrier: "This is not to be spoken of," and thus a door of understanding remained closed between us throughout the remainder of her life. It is her handwriting within a book authored by one of her older sisters that gives me a glimpse into her private struggles:

It was such a little sin and such a great big day.
That I thought the house would swallow it or the
wind blow it away. But the moment passed so
swiftly and the wind died out somehow. And the sin
that was a weakling once is a hungry giant now. I
wish there was some wonderful place in the land of
Beginning Again: Where all our mistakes and all
our heartaches, and all our error and sin could be
dropped like a shabby old coat at the door, and
never put on again.
I knelt to pray when day was done and prayed, 'Oh
Lord bless everyone. Lift from each sadden heart the
pain and let the sick be well again.' And then I

woke another day and carelessly went on my way; the whole day long I did not try to wipe the tear from any eye . . . Yet once again when day was done I prayed, 'Oh Lord, bless very one.' But as I prayed into my ear there came a voice that whispered clear, 'Please now my child before you pray whom have you tried to bless today? God's sweetest blessings always go with hands that serve him here below.' And then I hid my face and cried, 'Forgive me God. I have not tried. Please let me live another day. And I'll live the way I pray.'

When I read these words, I come to an understanding of a woman who suffered less at the hands of others than from an unforgiving ego fettered to her own grief, shame, remorse, and guilt. Therefore, I have become acquainted with a woman whose own suffering blinded her to the threads of grief and loss my three-year-old self had previously woven into a tapestry of  death and to the subsequent re-weaving of the incongruence between my father's going to heaven, my brother's disappearance, the baby's death, and the near-drowning of my older sister and I. Two weeks after my grandmother declared the baby dead, my infant sister—but not my father or my brother—returned to the family.

Thus, one false belief in a series of untrue concepts begot a childhood paradigm of ignorance derived from hearts and minds closeted by anxiety, shame, guilt, and anger. Another aspect to this recollection is the total absence of my mother within the series of events surrounding my sister's birth, death, and resurrection. It is as if she was seated in the audience, unseen and unknown, while my grandmother, my baby sister, and I were string-puppets entangled by our individual kammic threads.

Unbounded love guards compassion against
turning into partiality,
Prevents it from making discriminations
by selecting and excluding,
And thus protects it from falling into partiality or
aversion against the excluded side.

~ Nyanapobika Thera

THE THRESHOLD OF STILLNESS

*May I find the Stillness within Silence so that I find
refuge within a "Cloud of Unknowing" that is
absent of greed, anger, and ignorance.*

This journey with *saldage* has brought me to a place and time in which to unweave and sort through the pseudo-beliefs I have simply, without question, absorbed through the lens of childhood fantasy and comprehension.   To begin this process is to reformulate beliefs through a process of mindfulness and analysis and then to know for myself, "These things are bad, blamable, censured by the wise; undertaken and observed, these things lead to harm and ill... These things are good, blameless, praised by the wise... These things lead to benefit and happiness."

It is not an easy undertaking to not simply believe what has been learned within family, school and church as well as conclusions reached through readings. The invitation to not simply follow tradition brings to the surface conflicts with compliance and opposition that come from an avalanche of values and guiding principles that outlines how I understand the roles and expectations of women.

To not adhere to that which was surmised within family stories about an ancestor, who upon seeing a swarm of locust "knelt in his patch of grain and pleaded with his

Maker to spare his wheat" and then saw them divide and not damage his remaining crops. Or within the story about the ancestor, who during a trip from New York to England, calmed the seas with a prayer, and while in England, after much fasting and prayer administered to a deaf and dumb boy who was subsequently healed.[9] To not simply believe opens a door of pondering about generations of family members who intimately knew powerlessness and insecurity, who eased their feelings of incompetence through prayer, and whose conceptions blinded them to their neighbors' plight.

To not simply believe that I must endure suffering is to reject the axiom that there is an absence of fundamental faith and goodness. To not adhere to the assumed abilities of ancestors frees me from the belief that a sincere act of making amends for my sins will open the doors to Shangri-La. To not simply draw upon scripture unbinds me to the shame that I don't have the faith – even of the size of a mustard seed – to be deeded as "good  and without sin" so what I wish for, even that which goes counter to nature's laws, will be granted. To ease the suffering within discontent is to not simply hold to be true that I am to acquiesce to pain until the final judgment of death, and only then will I be forever at peace, or forever condemned to an existence of even greater suffering.

To not simply believe opens my ears to the

---

[9] Clara Fullmer Bullock, *More than Tongue Can Tell* (1960).

incongruence within a belief in an all-knowing presence who, if not validated, punishes, absent of the grace within loving-kindness. To not simply believe brings a compassionate acknowledgment to the painful efforts to sway God into granting me my desires through bargaining, sacrifice, negation, and suffering, and to finally surrender with acceptance to "Thy will be done on earth as it is in heaven." To not simply believe sheds light upon the greed, aversion, and delusions that are intertwined into my conception of and relationship with life.

I do hold that my beliefs and the subsequent desire for their illusive promises of validation, forgiveness, or reunification have set me upon an unending path of suffering. These beliefs lead to harm and ill as they are like thorns that tear into my heart. This searing pain releases resentment intertwined with envy, awakens alienation, and denies me the essence of Christ's wisdom and loving compassion.

Christ stood before self-righteous anger and commanded that only the one without sin was to cast the first stone of punishment and, at another time and in the midst of his own suffering, sought forgiveness for those who "know not what they do." Within these written words, I hear compassion speaking for the suffering intertwined within anger ungoverned by moral shame and moral dread. Compassion is telling us how suffering, entangled into knots of mental, emotional, and social turmoil, deafens us to our guiding principles and blinds us to the horrors our moral shame will witness as it awakens from darkened ignorance.

The practice of the presence of God as being
comparable to that of consciousness
finally makes possible "full awareness" applied
to every thought, world, and deed.

~ Unknown

May I find the Equanimity that will lift a veil of shamed despair and acquaint me to the perceived and perceiver absent of greed, anger, and ignorance.

At the threshold of stillness within silence, the scent of mothballs signals the opening of a small steamboat trunk entrusted with long-forgotten memorabilia. Carefully placed upon a layer of women's 1930 era clothing are three stacks of yellow ribbon-tied envelopes. Within each are hand-written letters reminiscent of second grade penmanship inquiring, "Dear Mother, how are you? Fine I hope." On the left side is a stationery box filled with certificates of marriage, birth, baptism, and death intermingled with a child's brilliantly colored drawings. Beneath the box is a small silk sachet holding a solitary diamond engagement ring and an ivory locket. At the bottom of the trunk, children's books and wooden blocks with carved letters surround a miniature wooden rocking chair and a one-button eyed velvety-patched teddy bear. I become distracted from the remaining contents as black and white photograph images softly held within the folds of a woman's garnet silk dress glide in the air and scatter on the floor.

The photographic images are a visual memoir of a young family where trust once allowed two young sisters to roam free throughout a field of tall, yellowed grass. "How many days," my questioning mind wonders, "how many days were left before the decline of my father's health shifted the lights of a colorful present into the gray-shaded time of waiting?" Within this stillness of waiting, memory tells of a young child seeking solace through repetitive rocking behaviors and of a father's fragile heart enduring a turbulent wait for a donated aorta.

I hear compassion speak to my heart and I begin to feel how my father intuitively knew of my inner turmoil and of the tranquil stillness within rhythmic repetition. His gift of a rocking chair tells me some fifty years after his death of the multiple emotional and physical sufferings within his suffering, the interconnectedness of the suffering within the family, and of his wish to ease our suffering.

As the fabric of the dress glides between my fingertips, the shadow of grief that holds the memories of my son emerges from a compartment hidden within the trunk. An old fear awakens as the image of grief's blackened shadow looms over me with its death-filled abyss of intermingled condemnation, uncertainty, and emptiness. I feel the void that will consume me if I were to release the  eternal care of my son to its embrace. I come to know that I hold no trust that within death is compassionate loving-kindness. Awareness arises to tell me that as I run from grief with the anguish of powerlessness to protect the heart of my soul, like an addict running from her addiction, grief becomes even more insidious. In this undifferentiated chaos of anguish, fear, and mistrust, hope seeks for the magical garment that when donned will transform me into the Great Mother. It is faith that clings to the belief that as God witnesses this transformation, absolution and reconciliation would simultaneously subdue this impenetrable monster and return my son, whole with the spirit of life, to my care.

Every sensation that is experienced . . . is a spark.
There is no way that the fire from this spark
will cease to burn because we encounter it
anew every moment.
The point is to not put out the fire
but to stand back and make it useful.

~ Unknown

The Practice of Divine Reading

This yearning imprisons me to anguished desolation. I call upon disciplined courage to help me depart this state of mind and wait beside a tranquil pool of water, alone, with a redefined faith that leads to a benefit and happiness. Within this waiting, I hear an invitation to engage in the art of *Lectio Divina*, a very ancient Christian practice that has been kept alive in the Christian monastic tradition. *Lectio Divina*, a Latin term meaning "divine reading", is a practice that involves a slow, reflective reading of the Scriptures wherein one listens, reverently, for the still voice of God. This spiritual activity is one that includes mindfulness, meditation, insight, and contemplation.

The practice begins with quieting the mind and cultivating the ability to listen deeply. In the twelfth century, Guigo, a Carthusian monk, described the four stages he considered essential to this practice. He identified the first stage as *lectio* (reading) where the Word of God is read, slowly and reflectively. *Lectio* opens the door to understanding. The second stage is *meditatio* (reflection). When a word or a passage is understood, the text is memorized while the reader gently repeats the words. The repetition interacts with one's thoughts, hopes, memories, and desires. Through this process of rumination, the deepest aspects of self absorb the text's meaning. The image of the ruminant animal quietly chewing its cud was used in antiquity as a symbol of the Christian pondering the Word of God.

The third stage is *oratio* (response), during which thinking subsides and one engages in a dialogue with God. That is, there is a transcending of self with a power beyond oneself in such a way that the absorbed meaning transforms the self in a profound and deep manner. From this, conscience guides one to a life lived more fully and intently. The final stage of *Lectio Divina* is *contemplatio* (rest) where all thoughts, understandings, and meanings subside. One is invited to simply rest and listen in silence as one is embraced by God—home, once again.

Lectio Divina is not a goal-oriented practice in which one reaches though a step-by-step, technique-by-technique process. It is a journey that awakens me, as a lay person, to the arising and vanishing of thoughts and feelings, and to the ebb and flow between speaking and listening, between questioning and reflecting.

This meditative practice may be colored by an indecisive mind and a divided heart. This is a heart and mind overwhelmed and lost as a cloud of uncertainty and confusion blocks an intentional search of clarity. When one's mind is clouded over it is like seeing a reflection muddled by internal conflict and mistrust. To contain this uncertainty and confusion, one must first note its arising as it is appearing, "indecisiveness and dividedness is rising within me." As they are abandoned, "indecisiveness and dividedness is abandoned." While they fade, "indecisiveness and dividedness is ceasing within me." When they are gone, "there is no indecisiveness and dividedness within me."

When indecisiveness and dividedness cloud one's understanding, they are most effectively countered through the connection with a qualified teacher, an investment in time to study, as well as time engaged with noble friends and suitable conversations.

The Art of Healing Sounds and Colors may aid in the abandonment of a conflicted mind and heart. It begins with two long breaths each followed by a cleansing sigh. With your third in-breath, imagine purified energy rising from the earth into your heart. As you exhale, release the toxic energy in your heart with the sound *huhrrr* as you exhale. After three visualizations, imagine your body absorbing the color red with your next in-breath. As you exhale, release any negative energy with the sound *huhrrr* as you exhale.

The world views of Christianity and Buddhism converge with the suggestions that the sense of homesickness that arises and then fades may be a trace memory of wholeness, and that a sense of home will arise again, and again it will vanish. The Buddha said that the ultimate truth of things is directly visible, timeless and calling out to be approached and seen. This reality is always available to us, and that the place where it is to be realized is within oneself. The ultimate truth is not something mysterious and remote, but the truth of our own experience. It can be reached only by understanding our experience, by penetrating it right through to its foundations. This truth, in order to become liberating truth, has to be known directly. That is known by insight, grasped and absorbed by a kind of knowing which is also an immediate seeing.

Wakefulness naturally radiates out when we are not so concerned with ourselves and are able to truly acknowledge the interdependence and connectedness of all that is.

I feel an invitation to consider by simply being in the moment, I am home and it is here that I will find the trust that will allow me to place the care of my son, no, not ever to death, but into the grace of God's love.

A vow made creates
meaning in a new life
and
unsettles an old way of being.

IV

THE JOURNEY HOME

FIVE CATEGORIES OF SELF

*All mental and physical phenomena occur in
accordance with laws and conditions and if the
universe were otherwise, chaos and blind chance
would reign.*

~ Unknown

As I sort through the various threads of thought,
imaginings, memories and beliefs I have woven into a
tapestry that illustrates my companionship with *saldage*, I
come to see a life colored by attempts to evade or expunge
an underlying current of dissatisfaction. This discontent is
generally felt as a yearning for something undefined, or a
vague sense that things are not quite right. It comes in the
wake of the realization that dreams are unreachable, and
expectations only create more turmoil. Sometimes it erupts
as sorrow, grief, anguish, or despair. As a result, I question
where is the wellspring of this homesickness for a place, a
person, a time that cannot be?

Buddhist psychology seeks to uncover the truth of
human suffering and to find a path that leads to the
cessation of suffering. The first two truths speak of
suffering and its nature, while the third and fourth truths

outline a life path that will bring about the cessation of suffering.

The First Noble Truth

Suffering, as a noble truth, is this: Birth is suffering,
aging is suffering, sickness is suffering, death is
suffering, sorrow and lamentation, pain, grief and
despair are suffering; association with the loathed is
suffering, dissociation from the loved is suffering, not
to get what one wants is suffering — in short,
suffering is the five categories of clinging objects.
~ Setting Rolling the Wheel of Truth

The First Noble Truth nudges me out of my own immersion within the misery of suffering through its validation that suffering is a universal occurrence despite one's race, culture, or affiliations. Even those who say, "all's right with the world," are impacted by the constant state of flux within their life and thus experience anxiety.

To be born is to struggle with physical changes that occur in conjunction with developmental milestones, to feel the pain that accompanies physical and medical frailties, and to wrestle with the process of dying and with death itself. To be human is to be dissatisfied with the wanting and obtaining of that which is pleasant, to know the fading of initial pleasure, as well as to experience the discomfort of unpleasant sounds, sights, scents, tastes, physical sensations, and thoughts. To be open to life is to experience the range of human feelings, be it fear, anger, sadness, and joy. To be with others is to know the distress of — real or imagined and spoken or unspoken — inclusion and exclusion.

The first truth also extends these truths of suffering to the unsatisfactory nature and general insecurity inherent in the law of impermanency. That is, all the phenomena of existence whatsoever, even the awe-inspiring and the horrifying, are subject to change and dissolution. Those who know the pleasures found within substances also are acquainted with the unease that accompanies excess. We all intimately know the truth of this impermanency in our longings to feel emotionally close to others, which soon changes into a yearning for separation. Consequently, without exception discontent does arise.

The eyes will not see that which breaks the heart.

Suffering is clinging to the illusion of an unchanging self; that is, to a belief there is a permanent self within the ongoing process of physical and mental occurrences which constantly arise, disintegrate, and dissolve. Hume wrote that self is a "bundle or collection of different perceptions, which succeed each other with inconceivable rapidity, and in a perpetual flux and movement." He further suggested that we create an idea of self as we processes our perception of events and things. Thus, there is not a tangible sense of self that remains consistent from one moment to the next. To desire, crave, or cling to a solid consistent self where there is only a changing psycho-physical complex is to create conditions that generate sorrow, grief, and dejection.[10]

The feeling of an "I" emerges from a reflection of the

---

[10] B. Russell, *A History of Western Philosophy* (New York, 1945).

stream of experiential consciousness that awakens when one becomes aware of being observed by an internalized watcher or seer who is felt but never known. Therefore, there is no denying that there is a wavering consciousness, an "I", that knits together streams of memories, thoughts, feelings, and interactions in such a manner that we are able to formulate an awareness of identity, continuity, striving, as well as an sense of ourselves and others.

Buddhist psychology suggests that the personal self that we experience, perceive, and conceive arises from five material and non-material elements: our bodies, feelings, perceptions, thoughts, and consciousness. These five categories of self introduce us to the nature of our being. We are the five and the five are us. Whatever we identify with, whatever we hold to as our self, falls within this collection. Together they generate the whole array of thoughts, emotions, ideas, and dispositions in which we dwell, "our world."

These five elements, neither singly or collectively, constitute any self, nor is there to be found any self apart from them. For example, when we hold a rose we see that it is composed of multiple elements, some tangible - leaves, stem, thorns, petals, stamens - and others intangible - scent, color, memories. If you were to remove any of these constituent parts, would you find an entity know as "rose"? As we are unable to find the rose in the absence of any one of these parts, we are also unable to find an enduring solid rose in any one of these elements. Hence the belief in a permanent solid self proves to be a mere illusion as we find a self riddled with gaps and ambiguities that appear coherent because of the monologue we keep repeating, editing, censoring, and embellishing in our minds.

The body, from the moment of birth until death, undergoes a continuous cycle of hunger and satiation. In the body as well in the mind, there is a constant process of grasping and rejecting; assimilating and dissimilating; and identifying and alienating. The body also hungers for human touch as equally as the mind thirsts for unique experiences, choice, and consciousness.

Feelings arise from the contact of our sense organs (ears, eyes, skin, nose, tongue) with the world outside ourselves as well as out of the interactions of the thinking mind and mental objects, including ideas, images, memories, and discursive thoughts. Feelings that arise are experienced as either pleasant, negative, or neutral. If what is experienced is felt to be positive, then slumbering feelings that range from attachment to greed awaken. We then become motivated to seek, experience, and retain the forms, sounds, smells, tastes, touches, and thoughts that we attribute to be the cause of our positive feelings. If what we experience is felt to be unpleasant, then there is an impulse to escape the form, sound, smell, taste, touch, or thought. The emotion that arises in response to negative feelings is designed to help us escape the object and is often felt as anxiety, fear, anger, aversion, or revulsion. In those situations where escape is prevented or delayed, then a desire for annihilation of the object or the self arises. If we experience neutrality, then we remain ignorant about the object due to our feelings of indifference.

Perception is the recognition of objects through their form, sound, taste, texture which over time we accommodate to fit prior experiences and assimilate into mental categories: tables, trees, people, stars, etc. Perception can be divided into three levels of knowledge. The first level of perception is similar to the experience of a child when she first holds a coin; that is, she is open to the sensual experience of the coin's weight, shape, color, scent, temperature, and texture. This same coin will be perceived by an adult's knowledge through the lens of its monetary value. Then there is a holder who perceives the coin through analytical knowledge similar to that of a chemist.

As a water-vessel is variously perceived by beings
Nectar to celestials is for a man plan drinking water
While to the hungry ghost, it seems a putrid ooze of
pus and blood
Is for the water serpent-spirits and the fish a place in
live in
While it is a space to gods who dwell in the sphere of
infinite space.
So any object, live or dead, within a person or
without —
Differently is seen by beings according to their fruits
of kamma.

~ The Buddha

Thoughts are like the potentiality of an apple tree to bear fruit; the potentiality cannot be found anywhere in the tree, but we know the potentiality is there when we see apple blossoms. This potentiality, an ongoing series of units, begins as the mind acknowledges an object and it's characteristics. From this contact, there is an affective response which energizes goal seeking and task completion.

Over time, these ongoing units formulate our habitual tendencies, dispositions, inclinations, obsessions, and self-referenced stories.

Also, within these mental states are layers of conscience, which serve to regulate our infantile desires, consider external judgment, and formulate moral and guiding principles.

Feeling, perception, and thoughts are to consciousness as softness, scent, and redness are to a rose. We have six different avenues of consciousness by which to be aware of our external world. Each of the senses provides us with a unique consciousness of its own; be it, visual, auditory, gustatory, olfactory, bodily, and mental. Ordinary consciousness is the state we are in prior to the practice of mindfulness of body, feelings, mind, and consciousness. Mind consciousness provides us with the discriminative deliberate faculty we become aware of as an "observing or watching mind" that is felt, but never known.

Consequently, the quality of our cognitive processing of the world around us depends upon unimpaired sense organs, an external visible form, and the act of attention. Generally though, our minds give greater attention to self-referenced stimuli. It is interesting to note how our eyes can pinpoint the letters that together form our name out of a page of text or the sensitivity to hearing our name over the rumble of a crowd.

But at this time, one wonders why does the First Noble Truth note that the five categories - body, feelings, perceptions, thoughts, and consciousness - are suffering? These categories are changing moment to moment, arising from conditions only to become conditions for something else with nothing substantial persisting throughout the arising and fading. Since the constituent factors of our being are always changing, utterly devoid of a permanent core, there is nothing we can cling to as a basis for security. There is only a constantly disintegrating flux which, when clung to in the desire for permanence, plunges us into suffering.

The problem is cognitive and so the solution is also cognitive.

The Four Foundations of Mindfulness

In walking, just walk. In sitting, just sit. Above all, don't wobble.

Bare attention is cultivated through a series of practices called "the four foundations of mindfulness", the mindful contemplation of body, feelings, thoughts, and consciousness. Mindfulness of the body is developed as a methodical meditative practice such as meditative walking or Tai Chi. Another practice is a general attitude of mindfulness and clear comprehension of one's movements throughout an average day.

Mindfulness begins with the breath. The first step begins with the notation of a long inhalation or exhalation of the breath as it occurs. The second is a notation of a short inhalation or exhalation as it occurs. One simply observes the breath moving in and out, observing it as closely as possible, noting whether the breath is long or short. As mindfulness grows sharper, the breath can be followed through the entire course of its movement, from the beginning of an inhalation through its intermediary stages to its end, then from the beginning of an exhalation through its intermediary stages to its end. This third step is called "clearly perceiving the entire body." The fourth step, "calming the bodily function", involves a progressive quieting down of the breath and its associated bodily functions until they become extremely fine and subtle.

The practice notes or observes the elements within every bodily act of seeing, hearing, tasting, feeling, thinking, smelling. Each should be noted as "seeing, seeing", "hearing, hearing", etc. as one discriminates between 1) an object, 2) consciousness of seeing, hearing, etc., 3) the function of the particular sense organ: eyes, ears, tongue, skin, mind, nose, or 4) the knowing of the image, sound, tastes, sensation, thought, scent.

In regards to body mindfulness, every kind of touch, either pleasant or unpleasant, is accompanied by a touch consciousness that feels or knows the touch as it occurs. With practice, we will come to know that each sensation of touch involves the skin, the impression of touch upon the skin, and the mind knowing of the touch.

Since our bodies at times feel stiff, tired, hot, numb, cold, ache, it is recommended that particular qualities of sensation should be acknowledged as "feeling stiff", "feeling tired", "feeling hot", etc. as the case may be.

Our touch consciousness awakens as we move about our days through a series of body movements and activities. The body can assume four basic postures—walking, standing, sitting, and lying down—and a variety of other positions marking the change from one posture to another. Mindfulness of the postures focuses full attention on the body in whatever position it assumes: when walking one is aware of walking, when standing one is aware of standing, when sitting one is aware of sitting, when lying down one is aware of lying down, when changing postures one is aware of changing postures. These practices should be noted and labeled as, "bending", "stretching", "walking", "breathing", "sitting", etc.

In regards to the series of mental activities that arise in conjunction with our bodily movements - thoughts and imaginations - each of these should be noted as "thinking" or "imagining" as the case may be.

Over time, with consistent practice, one will begin to notice that the mind lessens its tendency to wander and remains more attentive to the object of concentration. At the same time, there is an increased awareness of the body-mind relationship and an understanding of the multiple activities we undertake throughout the day to ease various discontents; that is, hunger, boredom, physical aches and pains, loneliness, inadequacy, worries, conflicts. This opens the door to knowledge that the dynamics within our mind-body structure are not governed by our desires. This is the beginning of insight into suffering.

What may interfere with one's mindfulness practice is one of the five hindrances. Sloth and torpor is a heaviness of mind equal to dullness, apathy, lethargy, or rigidity. When one is overcome with lethargy it is like trying to see the life below the surface of a pond that is covered with moss and water plants.

To become mindful of lethargy one must first accept its arising without sinking into its heaviness with, "fatigue is rising within me." As it is abandoned, "fatigue within me is abandoned." While it is fading, "fatigue is ceasing within me." When it is gone, "there is no fatigue present within me." To dispel dullness and drowsiness it is suggested that one visualize a brilliant ball of light, undertake brisk walking meditation, reflect on death, or meditate with a firm determination to break through this mental fatigue.

The Art of Healing Sounds and Colors may also assist with the abandonment of lethargy. This practice begins with two long breaths each followed by a cleansing sigh. With your third in-breath, imagine purified energy rising from the earth into your kidneys. As you exhale, release toxic energy in your kidneys with the sound *cherweeee* with your out-breath. After you have completed three complete visualizations, visualize your body absorbing the color dark blue with your next in-breath. As you exhale, release any remaining negative energy with the sound *cherweeee*.

The mindfulness of the postures illuminates the impersonal nature of the body. It reveals that the body is not a self or the belonging of a self, but merely a configuration of living matter subject to the directing influence of volition. This is insight into non-self.

To relinquish the root of pain; a person finds
happiness.
When she is gladdened, joy is born;
bring joyous in mind; the body becomes tranquil;
when the body is tranquil, she feels happiness;
and the mind of the person who is happy
is acquainted with single pointed tranquil
absorption.

~ Unknown

The feeling of yesterday is a present feeling... It is amazing to acknowledge the manner by which our ego holds onto our feelings and beliefs as if they were objects to possess or tangible entitlements to protect despite their potential to consume or destroy. It is as if feelings have the creative ability to create story lines and to take our mind hostage while formulating validation, rationalization, and justification for their continued presence. For example, anger once awakened by other feelings - such as, pride, jealousy, fear, or grief - seems to have an uncanny ability to recall historical events to justify its continued presence as well as to drawn upon an unlimited supply of resources to insure its survival.

A life well lived is a life in which there are multiple incidents in which one pauses for a moment or two, and through tears and words, releases the suffering intrinsic to the little deaths of ordinary life; a lost toy, a friend moves away, childhood fantasies fade into adolescent angst. Yet, when the death of a loved one or a betrayal of esteemed trust meets us at our doorstep, tears alone will not release us from the fountain's stream of confusion, rage, and anguish.

Therefore, when the deepest aspect of ourselves encounters loss through betrayal, it may be beneficial to inquire as to when we first felt disillusionment through deceit or injustice – that is when our young souls were naive, unscarred, and thus vulnerable. To ask, "How old do I feel I am at this moment?" may assist with the realization that unresolved losses do not fade away in the morning's light.

Wounds multiply as they slumber deep within our

souls, waiting to be released through the gift of a voice heard and an enlightened understanding. Yet, when life touches our wounds and hope encourages them to speak, there is a struggle between the ability to find words that truly convey the meaning of our suffering and a fear that our story will only drive others away and thus we will be abandoned in awakened despair.

Betrayal is a double-edged sword, in that to be betrayed by another may reflect one's naivety, anxieties, powerlessness or how one deceived self within the relationship through the negation of innate wisdom, relinquished self for alternative desires, or clung to an illusive fantasy. Therefore, the long and arduous path towards healing begins with the courage to step out of the dark emptiness of disillusionment and to acquaint oneself with a deeper consciousness and mature love that awaits in the arms of tranquil wisdom and compassionate loving-kindness.

Despite their sense of power, feelings are like bubbles, in that their arousal begins with a triggering event and their intensity and impact ends with the release of enveloped energy. The energy within our feelings can range from the intensity that we witness in a pan of rolling boiling water to the gentle movement of the sea foam as it brushes against the sand. Each individual bubble is ephemeral; our feelings are equally fleeting.

External objects trigger feelings. We perceive an object; we respond. A neutral object is labeled as threatening, ludicrous, sad, or beautiful - not as a consequence of thinking about the object - but in response to our considering and labeling seemingly instant behaviors:

anger, laugher, tears, or admiration. The mere memory or imagination of a particular object may stir a response. We may find ourselves angrier after thinking about an insult than at the moment of hearing the insult, or missing someone more after their death than we ever did during their lifetime.

William James noted that "we feel sorry because we cry, angry because we strike, afraid because we tremble, and not that we cry, strike, or tremble, because we are sorry, angry, or fearful, as the case may be. Without the bodily states following the perception, the latter would be purely cognitive in form, pale, colorless, destitute of emotional warmth. We might then see the bear, and judge it best to run, receive the insult and deem it right to strike, but we should not actually feel afraid or angry."[11]

Our feelings are expressed through nine primary affects: interest, happiness, guilt, shame, worry, fear, surprise, anger, sadness, dissmell, and disgust. Each of these feelings are experienced as having different shades of intensity, and known through an appraisal of our physical sensations; for example, increased heart rate, blushing, furrowed brow, dry mouth, shallow breathing, clenched jaw, butterflies in the stomach, and trembling knees and hands.[12]

Initial feelings activate emotions. Emotions in turn trigger thinking. Also, thinking stirs up feelings, which then can stimulate emotional reactions. Consequently, we sometimes confuse our feelings with our thinking process.

---

[11] William James, *The Principles of Psychology*, (New York, 1890), 450.

[12] For more information on words identified with body qualities, see Peter Levine, *Healing Trauma*

Feelings are generally put into sentences that begin with "I feel . . ." Thinking sentences begin with "I think . . ." or "I suppose . . ."

A good way to test if a sentence is a feeling sentence or a thinking statement is to change "I feel . . ." to "I think . . ." or to change "I think." to I feel . . ." (e.g., changing "I feel angry" to "I think angry"). If it makes more sense to say, "I feel . . .", it is probably more an expression of how one is feeling than what one is thinking.

Our mental qualities color the way we see the world; therefore, they are an integral aspect of our nature. Within Buddhist thought, these qualities are identified as either detrimental or beneficial. They have the potential to torment and comfort our minds and by extension people within our field of connection.

The importance in acquiring and using techniques that assist with the removal of detrimental thoughts is found within the analogy of the dandelion. That is, when thoughts arise seeds burst free like the wished-upon dandelion and replant themselves in our mental mind stores. Therefore, it is recommended that repetitive unwholesome thoughts be removed as if they were weeds by: embracing small incidents of positive memories, reflecting upon the negative consequences of these thoughts, shifting attention to specific body movements, letting go of the thought, and pushing them away. It is important to keep in mind that while the removal of unwholesome thoughts is instructed, the effective management of feelings is through the use of containment skills.

The subsequent emotional, practical, moral, or spiritual values we attach to feelings are determined by our own self talk that arises in conjunction with particular bodily sensations. Therefore, it is not the feeling itself, but the quality of our own mental responses that labels our feelings as good or bad. Hence there are feelings we enjoy and those we don't.

We acquaint ourselves with our feelings through particular physical sensations. We also begin to understand our emotions through our behaviors as noted by the "e" within "e-motion", the energy that impels motion. Our emotions are seen within the dance of closeness and distance within our relationships. We feel them as they propel us to join forces with others, to engage in various interests, to meet our personal needs, as well as to withdrawal and isolate from others.

We know them through behaviors undertaken to change a loved-one's alcohol or drug use or to bring about social justice. A significant property of an emotional system is that it translates basic energy into a set of clearly identifiable, predictable, and interrelated behavior patterns and feeling responses. Emotions are also the internal conflicts we experience when our behaviors and desires are incongruent. They direct us to reflect and re-examine our thoughts and actions, as well as dislodge us from self-immersion. Others we can reflect upon only after the dust settles due to the manner we were compelled to act by sudden urges or desires.

To repetitively abandon ourselves to the force of our emotions is indulgence. To defend ourselves from this natural process through denial, suppression, or repression is to swing to the extreme of asceticism. The middle way is to acknowledge that all of our feelings, thoughts and actions are intertwined and impacted by each of these three elements. Therefore, it takes an emotion to manage a feeling; that is, to channel our energy into acknowledging the sensation of a feeling as it arises, assigning to it a name, and observing it's fading. The process of acknowledging and naming a feeling contains the energy within the feeling, and thus the feeling loses its power to control, intimidate, and harm our lives.

Western psychology proposes that actions either are directed by thoughts which were awakened by feelings or awaken feelings which in turn stimulate thoughts. Consequently, there will be therapeutic interventions that include an exploration of one's thoughts, self-talk, to determine if chemical use is maintained through one's "addictive thinking." Other classifications of thoughts, including over-generalization, black-and-white, all-or-nothing, are also believed to impact one's feelings and subsequent actions. The alteration or removal of these cognitive imprints is seen to be an important component of a recovery plan.

Since nature abhors a vacuum, an effective therapeutic intervention will include a plan of action that fills the void of abstinence with ingredients that assist with the cessation of suffering, or with changes that assist with a positive lifestyle. Therefore, recovery will include an encouragement to remove addictive behaviors through the implementation of attendance to a Twelve-Step program.

Those who recognize emotional patterns within relationship systems understand the movements toward and away from substances as an attempt to manage chronic anxiety that arises from the opposing needs of togetherness and separateness. The movement towards substances is clearly, at times a movement away from significant others, and at other times utilized as a means to ensure time together. Anger and resentment are also at times directed towards objects and individuals when they are attributed as obstacles that block closeness with another. At other times, people will join with others in a unified front to enforce non-using behaviors.

Chronic substance use is also understood as validation that someone within the relationship has assumed total responsibility for the continuation of the relationship. This posture of over-functioning, which is driven by anxiety, is counter productive as it only serves to insure an under-functioning counterpoint. Clinical interventions developed through this perspective will seek to work with the person who is motivated to address her own emotional and relational functioning, as opposed to an intent to bring about change in the other.

> *The fountain of contentment must spring up in the mind and*
> *[she] who hath so little knowledge of human nature*
> *as to seek happiness by changing*
> *anything but [her] own nature will waste [her] life in fruitless*
> *endeavors and multiply the grief [she] wishes to remove.*
> ~ Samuel Jackson

These viewpoints are now being further extended through studies that investigate the communication system within the human nervous system. It is suggested that our nerve cells communicate with each other through the release of specific chemicals and that we affect the exchange of neurotransmitters through all of our behaviors—running, sleeping, reading, talking, thinking—as well as through what we ingest: food, prescribed and non-prescribed drugs, alcohol. These behaviors as well as bodily sensations stimulate our nerve cells to release chemicals which in turn influence our feelings, thoughts, and actions.

From this perspective, a therapist may recommend a combination of behavioral and cognitive interventions as well as education about the brain's functioning, changes in one's diet and exercise, and medication to assist with recovery.

Buddhist psychology, on the other hand, teaches that feeling is an inseparable concomitant of consciousness, since every act of knowing is colored by some affective tone. Thus feeling is present at every moment of experience; it may be strong or weak, clear or indistinct, but some feeling must accompany the cognition. It proposes that the initial sensation of a feeling is either a body or a mental impression arising through the uniting of our sense organs (eyes, ears, skin, tongue, nose, mind), an object, and consciousness. The initial impression at this stage as sight, sound, sensation, taste, odor, or imagination begins simply as a sensation and will either fade from awareness or be processed and identified as a pleasant, unpleasant, or neutral sensation.

What are the two feelings?
Bodily and mental images.
What are the three feelings? Pleasant, painful, and
neither-painful-nor-pleasant feelings. What are the
five feelings? The faculties of pleasure, pain,

gladness, sadness, and equanimity. What are the
six feelings? The feelings born of sense-impression
through eye, ear, nose, tongue, body, and mind.
What are the eighteen feelings? There are the six
feelings by which there is an approach [to the objects]
in gladness; and there are six approaches in sadness
and there are six approaches in equanimity.
What are the thirty-six feelings? They are six
feelings of gladness based on the household life and
six based on renunciation' six feelings of sadness
based on the household life an six based on
renunciation; six feelings of equanimity based on the
household life and six based on renunciation.
What are the hundred and eight feelings? They are
the thirty-six feelings of the past, they are thirty-six
of the future and there are thirty-six of the present.

~ The Buddha

With regard to the six senses, one distinguishes six kinds of feelings; feeling associated with seeing, hearing, smelling, tasting, bodily impression and mental impression. Each of our sense organs has a consciousness particular to it's functioning; that is, a hearing consciousness, seeing consciousness, smelling consciousness, tasting consciousness, feeling consciousness, or thinking consciousness. Our thinking consciousness arises as either discursive or visual images.

The coming together of these three elements (sense organ, object, and consciousness) is referred to as "contact." The oldest structure of our mind identifies this bodily contact as either a positive or negative sensation and the mental impression as gladness, sadness, or indifferent. Every conscious experience is colored by one of these three feeling qualities, for even indifference has a distinct quality of its own.

Feelings set into motion a process of recognition, engagement, and attention to a particular object. Therefore, our relationship with the world is determined by the absence or presence of an object and the quality our sense organs. Contact is the spark that energizes us to pursue, avoid, or be indifferent to sensory experiences due to the motivation to insure, establish, or reinstate physical or mental happiness.

> *What a person considers and reflects*
> *upon for a long time,*
> *to that his mind will bend and incline.*
> ~ The Buddha

Consequently, Buddhist psychology appears to clarify the relationship between an individual and drugs/alcohol as a process that begins when our sense organ ascertains the chemical or an object (pipe, needles, bar) associated with past use. This contact awakens positive, negative, or indifferent memories associated with prior use. The motivation to experience pleasure results in behaviors that ensure use through a mind engaged and focused upon obtaining the drug of choice.

Feeling Meditation

Buddhist psychology encourages a personal endeavor to see

if there is truth in the perspective that to be human is to be bombarded by the world through our six senses and that our suffering is linked to our cravings. Mindfulness invites us to become aware of our feeling's origins and to acquaint ourselves with their arising and ceasing. When we fail to acknowledge and identify feelings, they accumulate through a process of repression and concealment. Over time, this shield forms into layers of habit that are difficult to change as they generate more suffering.

To undertake a practice of mindfulness of feelings may shed light into the pain and turmoil within mental qualities such as pride, conceit, and jealousy that speaks of our ties to our ego. One may come to hear the voice of the suffering that comes from not knowing how to break habits that are self-defeating, not knowing how to change patterns that are misguided, not knowing how to find better, more creative, satisfying ways of being, not knowing how to rediscover an authentic life. One may come to see that the pushing away of desires is just as much a desire as having desires in the first place.

One of the contributions within the practice of mindfulness of feeling is its ability to teach a method of relating to one's own rage that is the psychic substitute of parental holding. This containment, with regular practice, will ease our suffering, open our hearts and minds to our finer emotions, and allow us to respond to life in a more natural and spontaneous manner.

When we feel a feeling we are not that feeling. If we change a feeling statement such as "I am angry" to "I feel anger," and then to "this feeling is anger; it is unpleasant; it too will fade; another feeling sensation is arising; this feeling is . . ." how may this change impact one's recovery?

In the early stages the mindfulness of feeling involves attending to the arisen feelings, noting their distinctive qualities: pleasant, painful, neutral. The feeling is noted without identifying with it, without taking it to be "I" or "mine" or something happening "to me." Awareness is kept at the level of bare attention: one watches each feeling that arises, seeing it as merely a feeling, a bare mental event shorn of all subjective references, all pointers to an ego. The task is simply to note the feeling's quality, its tone of pleasure, pain, or neutrality.

Yet as practice advances, as one goes on noting each feeling, letting it go and noting the next, the focus of attention shifts from the qualities of feelings to the process of feeling itself. The process reveals a ceaseless flux of feelings arising and dissolving, succeeding one another without a halt. Within the process there is nothing lasting. Feeling itself is only a stream of events, occasions of feeling flashing into being moment by moment, dissolving as soon as they arise. Thus begins the insight into impermanence, which, as it evolves, overturns the three unwholesome roots. There is no greed for pleasant feelings, no aversion for painful feelings, no delusion over neutral feelings. All are seen as merely fleeting and insubstantial events devoid of any true enjoyment or basis for involvement.

Feelings should be mindfully observed only when they occur; therefore, it is not advised to produce in oneself feelings intentionally, just for the sake of practice. An awakened and calm mind will find many opportunities to contemplate feelings at their primary stage.

Set the intention. For example, "May I be singularly

mindful of this feeling and without any reference to the faintest thoughts of "I" or "mine." To be aware of feelings without any reference to the ego will help to distinguish them clearly from the physical stimuli arousing them as well from the subsequent mental reactions to them.

Label the feeling. Become mindfully aware of the feelings when they arise with a clear distinction of them as pleasant, unpleasant or neutral, respectively. At this initial level of sensation there is no such thing as "mixed feelings."

Acknowledge craving and aversion. If a thought arises, "This is a pleasant feeling . . . I wish for more . . .", label this thought as "clinging". When thoughts arise such as "This does not feel good . . . I want it to end", note them as "aversion."

Silence your internal dialogue. Strive to be persistently mindful of the arising and passing away of every instant of the feeling wherever and however it is occurring. To know with clarity the vanishing point of feelings assists with the containment of feelings and decreases subsequent detrimental emotions, thoughts and behaviors that are habitually associated with a particular feeling.

Dedication of merit. End this contemplation by dedicating any good that came during your practice to the benefit of others.

This practice will ease the propensity of being carried away by our emotional cross currents of elation and dejection and gradually support our ability to be a presence of calm abiding. Therefore, remember and apply this practice whenever feelings are prone to turn into disturbing emotions.

Continued practice will result in a greater awareness of

the sublime states: compassion, loving-kindness, sympathetic joy, and equanimity. With the comprehension of each of these sublime states and discernment of their unique qualities, then one's meditation practice can be extended to include an intention to breathe in the understanding of a particular sublime state and to breathe out that same awareness. Each in and out breath is co-joined with a mindfulness that is ardent, alert, and steady as well as absent of greed and suffering.

While there are feelings that we enjoy and those we would rather not experience, they are simply sensations that have bubbled up into our consciousness in response to a trigger. They can be felt to be similar to waves flowing in and flowing out in a natural rhythm.

What may impact one's practice is one of the hindrances, an intention to experience desirable experiences. Desire pulls a person away from their reflection as their attention is drawn towards that which carries an implied promise of pleasure.

To effectively contain desire one must first acknowledge its presence without distraction by noting, "an intention to experience desirable experiences is rising within me." As it is abandoned, "an intention to experience desirable experiences is abandoned." While it fades, "an intention to experience desirable experiences is ceasing." When it is gone, "there is no intention to experience desirable experiences within me."

When our minds are filled with desire, it is like trying to focus upon one's reflection in a bowl of water filled with multi-colored precious stones. It is suggested that the meditation on impermanence may assist with containing the pleasure seeking mind. To remove the desire for excitement and new experiences one is encouraged to mediate on impure objects, to guard the sense doors, to eat in moderation, and to engage in noble friendships and suitable conversations.

The Art of Healing Sounds and Colors may also assist with the abandonment of desire. This practice begins with two long breaths each followed by a cleansing sigh. With your third in-breath, imagine purified energy rising from the earth into your lungs. As you exhale, release the toxic energy in your lungs with the sound *see-ahhhh* as you exhale. After your third visualization, imagine your body absorbing the color green with your next in-breath. As you exhale, release any remaining negative energy with the sound, *see-ahhh*.

The Second Noble Truth

The origin of suffering, as a noble truth, is this: It is
the craving that produces renewal of being
accompanied by enjoyment and lust, and enjoying
this and that; in other words, craving for sensual
desires, craving for being,
craving for non-being.
~ Setting Rolling the Wheel of Truth

James noted that desire, wish, and will are states of mind common to everyone: "We desire to feel, to have, to do, all sorts of things which at the moment are not felt, had, or done. If with the desire there goes a sense that attainment is not possible, we simply wish; but if we believe that the end is in our power, we will that the desired feeling, having, or doing shall be real; and real it presently becomes, either immediately upon the will or after certain preliminaries have been fulfilled."[13]

The craving for sensual desire is understood as a yearning for sights, sounds, smells, tastes, and touches that are pleasant as well as a longing for wealth, power, position, and fame. Craving is known by an addict as a need to find a substance that once promised euphoria and now only postpones suffering. It is known in the anxiety that comes with thoughts about losing what one has and the fear of the emptiness that follows a loss. It is seen in the vague depression within boredom which gives energy to the

---

[13] William James, *The Principles of Psychology*, (New York, 1890), 486.

creation of a life filled with excitement and challenges.

The craving for being is manifested in the human desire to know self, to know an identity. Various schools of Western thought within psychology, theology, and philosophy have set forth ideas of what composes the self. As James noted, "In its wildest possible sense, a man's Self is the sum total of all that he can call his, not only his body and his psychic powers, but his clothes and his house, his wife and children, his ancestors and friends, his reputation and works, his lands and horses, and yacht and back-account. If they wax and prosper, he feels triumphant; if they dwindle and die away, he feels cast down."[14]

James divides self into four classes: the spiritual Self, material Self, social Self, and the pure Ego. The Spiritual self is the entire stream of our personal consciousness, or the present 'segment' or 'section' of that stream. It is the awareness we have of an innermost self in which we become conscious of within the moment and in the collection of such moments throughout our lifetime. It acts like a half-silvered mirror in that it allows us to reflect upon our past, gaze into our present and with a shift in our gaze, glimpse into an imaged future. It directs us towards and away from objects in the external world.

The body is the realm that encircles the spiritual self. In each of us certain parts of the body seem more intimately ours than others. The union of my body with my mind provides me with an identity that I reference to as mine. This mind-body matters to me. It's functioning impacts the quality of my life as well as my survival. The symmetry of

---

[14] William James, *The Principles of Psychology*, (New York, 1890), 291.

the left side of my body with that of my right illustrates uniqueness and beauty. My ego is invested in all the material elements that together form this body.

This material self extends from the body to our clothing. I adorn my body in a fashion that serves to protect as well as to confirm my sense of identity and role assumption. Extending outward from my clothing is my family. Each of us knows of the sense of loss of our very selves when a family member dies. We feel shame when someone in our family acts outside our moral compass. If we deem a family member has been insulted we feel an anger at least equal to that when we feel insulted.

From the family our selves extend to our homes and then to the various objects we collect: furniture, automobiles, art, electronic devices. These objects that we take possession of become extensions of our identity. The theft of one's car can bring about a sense of a shrinking self, "a partial conversion of ourselves to nothingness."

Our social self is created out of our need to be acknowledged by others as well as to feel that others see us in a favorable light. One of the cruelest punishments we impose on others is expel them or to treat them if they do not exist.

We have as many social selves as there are people who recognize us and carry an image of us in their minds. Different aspects of our selves are shown to different groups of people; therefore, the self our children know is not shown to our coworkers or the self shown to our minister is not the same as the one shown to a sales clerk. We are motivated to protect the images we believe people have of us. From this variable sense of different selves may be a discordant splitting when one person becomes acquainted with an aspect that is known elsewhere.

Ortega y Gasset wrote that a person's self is not a separate entity from the environment and that self is formulated through a dynamic interaction and interdependence of a person's inner being and her life's journey. Therefore, each of us seek our own truth and what we see, believe, and/or know of our ultimate self no other self can perceive or comprehend. Kaplan suggested that the Kabbalist did not view the body as the self or the three things identifiable with the self - the body, mind, and soul - as the self. He stated that these three things are known by us to be "mine", but the ultimate self is something more profound than what is possessed.

Kaplan furthered his discussion of the self with the suggestion that the ultimate self is a sense of volition. It is this intangible will which has us do whatever we decide to do. When we think, we must will our self to think, "it is the 'I' which tells the mind to think." We are unable to identify a tangible "I"; therefore, to imagine the source of will, the ultimate self, is to become aware of nothingness.

Russell indicated that Aristotle understood will to be the ultimate source of all movement and that we identify that which is alive from other things by the fact that they can move of themselves. The 'nature' of a thing, Aristotle said, is in its end, that for the sake of which it is alive. Therefore, drawing upon this perspective, self is like an acorn. That is, an acorn is "potentially" an oak tree.

Friedman wrote that the "rise of the existential, and perhaps biological category of self" is a part of the evolutionary emotional process that had its beginnings when the first eukaryotic cell separated itself in the process of reproduction. He further noted that from a system's perspective, self is "not a concept, it is a dynamic reality capable of maturation."

Friedman further noted that without immunologic systems, there would be no existential category of self since the immune system is basically the capacity of an organism to distinguish self from non-self. Therefore, during the initial stage of development during the 40 weeks of gestation, it could be understood that the development of the self necessitates an awareness by a mother-to-be of the developing person within her womb and the fetus's sense of the mother.

The separation of the newborn from the mother at birth is followed by a psychological fusion with mother, normal infantile autism. This first phase of development of the self is followed by symbiosis where the mother is seen as a partner and not just an interchangeable part. Eventually, within the process of separation/individuation, as the child moves away from symbiotic forms of relating, is the foundation where the child begins a knowing of self which is separate from others.

Within each of these separate schools of thought, self is associated with the manifestation of energy; that is, striving, dynamic, seeking, change, volition, will, nature, separation, reflection, and motion.

A significant property of an emotional system is that it translates basic energy into a set of clearly identifiable, predictable, and interrelated behavior patterns and feeling responses. An emotional system is sufficiently powerful to be able to effectively "program" its members to respond in certain prescribed ways. Therefore, family members who are bound together within an emotional field, as well as the family system as a whole identity, has discernible, predictable, and interrelated behavior patterns; i.e., conflict, emotional cutoff, triangles, and over/under functioning.

Brown wrote that "the family system is driven by emotional forces; in part that is why it is so important to the development of a sense of self. The emotional forces within the family will move to incorporate a third person to stabilize the dyad(s) within the system. The higher the anxiety within a family system and/or the lower the differentiation, the more intense the automatic triangling. It is through the process of emotional triangles that "we all tend to come out of our family of origin having particular postures or positions vis-à-vis our parents."

Friedman's discussion of the self and non-self further suggest that self is born from the anxiety associated with the conflict between self and non-self. If a family system's level of chronic anxiety was low enough to encourage differentiation, a functional outcome of this conflict between self and non-self would be a less reactive movement away from mother and a positive attachment between father and child. This ideal threesome would make room for an infant to begin an awareness of self with self, self with mother, self with father, and self with others.

In sum, self is an evolutionary movement towards potentiality that originated within our individual family's emotional system. Thus, the absolute nature of self is in an ongoing process of growth and development. The degree by which we are to feel self as a constant is related to our ability to correctly identify and predict our own behavior patterns and feeling responses within the ebb and flow of emotional systems.

Our ultimate self can only be perceived moment by moment through an intentional mindfulness to differentiate between that which we define as "mine" (my body, thinking, feelings, perceptions, awareness, will, and family) and that which we, through our feeling and thinking process, defines as non-self.

Consequently, a knowing of self reflects how we and our childhood family understood and accepted the natural and opposing pulls for united togetherness and separate individuality, managed the inherent anxiety within this essential and inseparable part of an ever-evolving process of separation and union, and adjusted to ongoing life-cycle and situational changes.

The Ego asserts, "I am the same self that I was yesterday." The ego is the aspect of the self that knits together the self of today with the self of yesterday. It weaves aspects of our selves together – our memories, feelings, thoughts – and brands them "mine." This form of branding sees a resemblance among the continuum of experiences and thus constitutes the real and verifiable "personal identity" which we feel. We cannot realize our present self without simultaneously feeling the experience of thinking, or feeling the body's actual existence at the moment.

Feelings arise when the ego, the perceiver of my self, comes in contact with objects and people that are important to me due to the inclusion of them as an aspect of self, the degree of value I have assigned to them, or the stories they awaken. I can become acquainted with my ego through it's

"I'm superior, I'm unique, I'm inferior" responses to external and internal stimuli. Objects that my ego defines as indicators of my self - my body, my thoughts, my beliefs, my family, my country - are responsible for the arising of powerful visceral reactions that determine the quality and direction of my interactions with others.

My ego locates me in the center of the universe; it seeks self-confirmation, and separates the world into classifications of "I" and "other." It validates Friedman's notation that that our existential category of self arises from our immune system in that it is designed to distinguish self from non-self. Therefore, my ego clings to all that messages a consistent, solid "I." It rejects the perspective that the central core of my being is not an unchanging soul but a life-current, an ever-changing stream of energy that is never the same for two consecutive seconds. The Buddha asserts that the self, considered as an eternal soul, is a delusion, and when regarded from that ultimate standpoint it has no reality; it is only within this delusion of selfhood that ultimate suffering can exist.

This natural propensity to place ourselves in the center of the universe suggests that the ego is a manifestation what is referred to as the "old brain." The feelings and behaviors of humans that are linked with searching for food, fighting, protecting ourselves and others, being affectionate, reproducing, and caring for our children are believed to originate from the oldest parts of the human brain. This "old brain" serves to ensure human survival and is associated with the impulsive, repetitive, instinctual, and intuitive aspects of our behavior.

It is the prefrontal cortex that is the newest and most

highly developed part of the human brain. This "new brain" operates on thought and provides us with the resources to be introspective and thus reflect upon the beneficial and detrimental consequences of our feelings, thoughts and actions.

It is suggested that there is a reciprocal relationship between the old and the new. Yet, since the old preceded the new, it will, during times of heightened anxiety, dominate how we perceive, process, and respond to what is identified as a threat to the various aspects of self. At these times we are governed more by how we feel and less by how we think.

It is difficult to comprehend how the energies invested in defining, validating, protecting, and maintaining the self would shift with a rage against one's own integrity and one's own life. Everyone at some time or other has experienced negative feelings that were so intense that the mind sought to eradicate that which was identified as accountable for the suffering without regard to what should take its place. In this state of mind there can unquestionably be genuine thoughts, and genuine acts, of suicide, spiritual and social, as well as bodily. Anything, anything, at such times so as to escape the pain and to not be, "God, make me into a stone." But such conditions of suicidal frenzy are pathological in their nature and run counter to everything that is regular in the life of the Self in man.

When we distance from loved ones through emotional or physical distance or with the statement, "you are now dead to me", this is a semi-intentional annihilation of self. It tells us of the degree of emotional fusion within families and a cutting away of the material self. To see oneself through lens of criticism, guilt, and negation are mini-acts of eradication of self. To withdraw and alienate oneself from society is an act seeking a form of non-being.

If one discerns that an object is acting as a preventative to obtaining something desired - possession, fame, validation, intoxication, power, inclusion, sensual gratification - then anger and hatred will be directed toward the blocking agent. Even if the blocking agent is self, the desirous ego will view self as an object and thus be free to abuse self, debase self, make self suffer and derived sadistic satisfaction from the suffering directed upon the self.

Freud indicated that an individual's super-ego is the internalization of parents, teachers, admired public figures, or high social ideals. It often manifests itself through guilt or shame and in answering to internal criticism develops extraordinary harshness and severity towards the self, "If we turn to melancholia first, we find that the excessively strong super-ego which has obtained a hold upon consciousness rages against the [self] with merciless violence as if it had taken possession of the whole of the sadism available in the person concerned . . . What is now holding sway in the super-ego is, as it were, a pure culture of the death instinct, and in fact it often enough succeeds in driving the [self] into death."[15]

An alcoholic may assert that the choice to drink is a manifestation of choice as well as a legal right. To surrender to the authority of another, despite the multiple costs incurred by continued use, is to lose "face" as well as the identity, entitlement and inclusion formulated through

---

[15]Peter Gray, ed., *The Freud Reader* (New York, 1998), 654.

drinking. While intoxication is an act of self annihilation, it has the potential to be the lesser of the two evils when faced with the multiple losses one encounters at the initial stages of recovery; i.e., giving up using friends, changing leisure and recreational activities, relinquishing rituals and customs, challenging thinking patterns.

If the only way to maintain the self is to lose others,
then the ordinary child will give up self.
~ Abraham Maslow

CESSATION

The Third Noble Truth

Cessation of suffering, as a noble truth, is this: It is remainderless fading and ceasing, giving up, relinquishing, letting go and rejecting, of that same craving.

~ Setting Rolling the Wheel of Truth

My discontent occurs in conjunction with the misery within my emotional, physical, and mental pain; within my efforts to modify, resist, and avoid change; within the continuity of my past endeavors upon my present and future; within the loss of loved ones, fame, pleasure, and praise; within efforts to suppress and conceal; and within attachment, anger, and closed mindedness and closed-heartedness.

If I wish to no longer suffer, the Buddha's words suggest that it is I who needs to open my mind to the noble truth that *saldage* follows the laws of impermanence, suffering, and un-self. It is I who keeps the wellspring of *saldage* flowing through my attachment, anger, and closed-mindedness and closed-heartedness.

The Buddha teaches that there is one defilement which gives rise to all the others, one root that holds them all in place. This root is ignorance. Ignorance is not mere absence of knowledge, a lack of knowing particular pieces of information. Ignorance can co-exist with a vast accumulation of itemized knowledge, and in its own way it can be tremendously shrewd and resourceful. As the basic root of suffering, ignorance is a fundamental darkness shrouding the mind. Sometimes this ignorance operates in a passive manner, merely obscuring correct understanding about impermanence, suffering, and non-self. At other times it takes on an active role: it becomes the great deceiver, conjuring up a mass of distorted perceptions and conceptions which the mind grasps as attributes of the world, unaware that they are its own deluded constructs. In sum, ignorance is one of the fundamental factors for suffering.

How does the comprehension of all phenomena as impermanent and impersonal begin to help me release the suffering within *saldage*? Impermanence is a two-sided coin. To know that each moment is fleeting, as all form and matter arises and vanishes at every moment of contemplation, nudges me into an awareness that it is in my best interest to cherish the welcomed moment that is arising, as it too will fade. To recall impermanence while overwhelmed by the confusion, anger, and despair that arises as one's world is crumbling amidst a loud whisper; "this shearing pain will be felt forever!" eases through an embrace that responds, "No. Nothing is forever; this too shall pass."

To be human is to cling to a sense of identity and to once again plunge myself into a cycle in which mind chases dimensions of self as they arise and fade, without a trace. The value in understanding suffering through this lens is to validate the unconscious drive to formulate an identity that seeks confirmation of being through a enduring spiritual Self, material Self, social Self, as well as an ego which differentiates the world into "mine" and "not mine."

To remain chained to the suffering within critical and unforgiving guilt is liken to an animal tied to a post, circling around and around a severe and rigid ego. Freedom from this cycle begins with the comprehension that some of my suffering arises from moral principles that were drawn from attachment to misconstrued family, cultural, and religious mythologies. There is a slow unweaving of this ignorance from a delusional self-referenced identity of a "sinner who misses the mark" with the comprehension that there is no concrete permanent self upon which to attach labels. These concepts help to clarify the purifying power of remorse through a new understanding of behaviors and identification with particular labels with a whisper to self, "On that particular day I was acting in such a manner that is incongruent with my guiding principles, values, and morals. I regret this action and am committed to a different course of action. May I also embrace the understanding that my behaviors are not rigid and consistent and thus relinquish this label placed upon me today. May I know the joy that arises as remorse and guilt fade away and may I release the merit within this joy."

> *High winds do not last all morning.*
> *Heavy rain does not last all day.*
> *Why is this? Heaven and earth!*
> *If heaven and earth cannot make things eternal,*
> *How is it possible for man?*
>
> ~ Tao Te Ching

Analytical & Stabilizing Meditation

A meditative practice that concentrates on the breath, with no understanding accompanying it, such as the understanding of impermanence, of ongoing change, and no solid me as the controller or observer, brings about a state of tranquility, but it will not bring a cessation to the suffering within *saldage*. A meditative practice that leads to the cessation of suffering includes the practice of analytical meditation followed by stabilizing meditation.[16]

Within this personal undertaking, analytical meditation begins with the mental features of investigating and scrutinizing. For example, throughout this writing, I have focused deeply into the personal meaning of *saldage* and by examining this metaphysical search for something, someone, or someplace that "cannot be." I have identified what it is that if relinquished would bring about a cessation of the suffering inherent in this sense of homesickness (It is important to note within this process the "I feel" is not to be refuted as there is an I which speaks of a relationship I that is not to be negated).

Through reflection I have become aware of the emergence of a cluster of physical sensations from my stream of experiential consciousness. Together with the awareness of this particular cluster of physical sensations is the identification of a feeling I have labeled as "homesickness for a place, person, or time" and the creation of a story about an I who is displaced and lost.

From this point, I ask of myself, "What are the defining characteristics of a person who is displaced and lost?" I inquire if I have had these characteristics since my conception. I then discern if my relationship with all living beings, from my spouse to the robin outside my house, is

---

[16]Alex Berzin, *The Two Truths,* http://www.talkingbuddhism.com (2005).

limited to and defined by these characteristics. In other words, have I always been displaced and lost, and does every living being relate to me as a displaced and lost person?

I come to the conclusion that the answer to both questions is no. I now hear an encouragement to release the story line that arises from my false identification with "I am displaced and lost." In conjunction with the release of this story line is the subsequent letting go of the construct of yearning for a person, place, or time. Within the emptiness that accompanies this release arises a consciousness of feeling - sadness intertwined with loneliness. To find that to simply acknowledge this particular cluster of physical sensations with "sadness and loneliness is arising" and to resist the urge to identify with these feelings releases me from the wellspring of suffering within the idea of *saldage*.

I am now free to concentrate on that discernment of myself as being freed from this metaphysical search, and to focus on this inferential understanding and to concentrate on discerning the impermanence of sadness and loneliness. This is the discriminating awareness that arises from meditating.

With stabilizing meditation, I focus solely upon being presently mindful without actively discerning it in detail. Thus, I concentrate on the feelings that arise with a mental factor of firm conviction to release the concept of self as displaced and lost. With this type of mediation, I rid myself of the tendency to ruminate and to be stuck in the various story lines that arise in conjunction with feeling sad and lonely.

Thus you must train yourself: "In the seen there will just be the seen; in the heard, just the heard; in the reflected, just the reflected; in the cognized, just the cognized." . . . when in the seen there will be to you just the seen; . . . just the heard; . . . just the reflected; . . . just the cognized, then . . . you will not identify yourself with it, you will not locate yourself therein. When you do not locate yourself therein, it follows . . . this will be the end of suffering.

~ The Buddha

Stabilizing mediations provide the medium by which I open myself to feel and absorb the idea of what it means to be emotionally connected with others and to formulate the idea of having a place that feels like home. The idea is a representation through words, an image, or a feeling, but with a meaning associated with the specific representation.

From a Western point of view, representing something with words and focusing on them is an "intellectual" process, while representing something through a feeling or image and focusing on it is an "intuitive" process. Both of these are conceptual and both need to be accompanied with correct understanding of what the words mean or what the feeling or image means.

Therefore, to be able to digest the understanding of being freed from my identification with *saldage*, I bring myself home through mindfulness, acknowledge the feelings of being emotionally connected with others, embrace and release trace memories of wholeness as they rise and fade, and with firm conviction absorb these intentions. In Western terms this is a visceral understanding. When this visceral understanding is accompanied by constructive emotions such as appreciation, I will be emotionally moved by this comprehension. This can bring about transformation. This transformation occurs nonlinearly; it is experienced as circular, sweeping, moving in and out.

The observer of this process follows the ebb and flow of my thoughts, accepts their occurring, and then lets them go through the act of returning to an object of my attention. This continual process of drifting from and returning to the present moment with nonjudgmental self-acceptance and self-compassion leads me to an understanding of single-pointed tranquil absorption.

Consequently, tranquility meditation is not about one's ability to remain focused upon an object of attention. It instead is the process of becoming aware of one's intrusive thoughts and feelings without acting upon them and returning, again and again, to the mindfulness that illuminates a healing-path that leads to the cessation of suffering.

If the clear light of mindfulness is present,
there is no room for mental twilight.

~ Nyanaponika Thera

The Fourth Noble Truth

The way leading to cessation of suffering,
as a noble truth, is this:
It is simply the noble eightfold path,
that is to say, right view,
right intention; right speech, right action,
right livelihood, right effort,
right mindfulness, right concentration.
~ Setting Rolling the Wheel of Truth

The Noble Eightfold Path is the middle path between two life-style extremes; one a life of intention to fulfill sensual desires and the other, a life of self-torment. This path divides into three branches, wisdom, morality, and diligence which when traveled brings one to a greater understanding of suffering and the cessation of suffering.

The figurative expression "path" does not imply that suffering ceases as one advances step by step in sequence after successfully understanding and implementing each of the eight "rights." What I have found is that to emerge from the darkness of despair requires a right intention to be guided by the principles of right mind, speech, action, and livelihood. The degree by which this intention is successful frees me to live a life with less tension and discontent, and thus I am able to engage more fully in understanding the concepts of right mindfulness and concentration. The containment and slow eradication of the five hindrances grants me the power of acquaintance to single-pointed tranquil absorption through a daily meditative practice, as well as through a personal investment in time to read and study various schools of thought.

Right view is forever impermanent as my transitory comprehension undergoes a transformation with each new encounter, each spark.

Dedication of Merit

As I bring this endeavor to define a healing-path to a close, I would like to share the merit I found while on this journey.

The first stone: become acquainted with the intrinsic power within generosity, gratitude, compassion, loving-kindness, equanimity, and sympathetic joy. Use their inherent strength to abandon detrimental mental qualities and experience the subsequent easing of suffering.

The second stone: familiarize yourself with the inherent strength within intention; that is, each morning define for yourself a small goal to strive for that day with the knowledge that the characteristics of each daily intention accumulates and formulates the meaning and purpose of your life.

The third stone: introduce yourself to the innate vitality of acquaintance with the knowledge of and experience with a presence that transcends your ego and nourishes your divine "I"-in-self.

The fourth stone: feel the influence within the natural aspect of prayer that releases the consequential merit of your actions, speech, and thoughts to the benefit all living beings.

The fifth stone: know the innate authority of remorse

that directs you to acknowledge when specific action, speech, and thought are incongruent with personal moral and guiding principles, to set forth the intention to not repeat the offense, and to release detrimental thoughts, including regret, shame, guilt, resentment, justifications, rationalizations. Feel the release of being freed from an abusive ego and to a self-centered attitude that has the inclination to neglect others.

The sixth stone: gift yourself the eloquence within simple acts of kindness absent of expectation: release your merit; share your talent, expertise, or knowledge; surrender your wants for another's need; greet each person with a half smile.

The seventh stone: be attentive to the influence present within a daily mindfulness practice that acquaints you to a state of tranquil single-pointed concentration.

We lose control of our behaviors at the moment of performance.
They inevitably return to us as our due heritage.

A
Meditative
Journey
with
Saldage

RESOURCES

ECHO AND NARCISSUS: EGO'S ATTACHMENT

Once upon a time when the world was young, sages believed that all of the elements in the heavens and on the earth were connected; therefore, they looked to the sun, moon, stars, and planets for answers to life's meaning and purpose. They saw how a breeze - silently and gently - guided a leaf in its autumn journey and how its dance - silently and gently - also altered the sojourn of the breeze. They saw gods and goddesses in the heavens, the passing of the seasons, the sounds and life of the forests, and the thunderous seas. They understood these supreme beings as powerful presences, each defined by unique attributes and limited by human-like frailties. Gradually, stories arose to tell of how life's challenges and triumphs were affected by and affecting the moods of, squabbles between, and relationships among these heavenly forces.

It was during this time that spirits of nature known as nymphs inhabited mother earth's rivers, forests, mountains, meadows, and glens. One named Echo, who loved a mortal named Narcissus, was known by all for her beauty and incessant babbling. That is, until the day Hera, the goddess of marriage, became enraged when she realized how Echo's chattering distracted her while she was intent upon learning the truth about Zeus' relationship with the mountain nymphs. Hera declared that any further sound that came from Echo would be - not a voice that formulated from within her - but the resounding last words of another.

Stripped of her ability to captivate Narcissus through the use of her enchanting sounds, Echo silently watched for him at the forest edge. One day he became separated from his friends; she heard him inquired, 'Is anyone here?' Hidden among the branches, she could only reply with a resounding, 'Here? . . . here?' Narcissus, in return, countered with a demand, 'Come!' Echo stepped out of the bushes with her arms outstretched and responded, 'Come! . . . come!' Narcissus turned his back to the sight of her as he heard her repeating insistence and retorted, 'I will die before I give you power over me!' Echo standing alone, exposed, in the clearing rejoined, 'I give you power over me, power over me.'

Helpless shame overcame Echo; she withdrew into the trees to hide among the rocks. One nymph, feeling the pain within Echo's unrequited love and failing to engage her in play, voiced a prayer, 'may he who loves not others love himself.' Nemesis, goddess of righteous anger, heard the prayer and pronounced, 'so be it that he who fears the sound of love sees the essence of his own love.'

So it came to be that when Narcissus bent over a clear pool of water and gazed upon his reflection, he fell deeply in love with the image before him. Yet, while the image that Narcissus gazed upon was his own, he identified his reflection as a beautiful living water-spirit possessing the attributes of the beautiful god, Apollo. When he moved to embrace his beloved, the image disappeared. He attempted to entice the image to no longer flee from his touch nor his tears with a silent appeal, 'Tell me why you flee from me.' Silence was the response. He soon came to understand that if he remained still and silent his beloved, who visually reciprocated his love, would not depart.

It has been told that Echo, muted by Narcissus' silence, remained next to him as he remained at the edge of the pool. In time, she turned into stone and he lost his color, his vigor, his beauty, and eventually his own life. As he rode the ferry across the Stygian river, he fell into the water never to be found by the water nymphs. Today when Spring begins to awaken barren lands, humans have chance encounters with Narcissus when he appears as a purple flower embraced by white leaves.

Attachment - One of the four near enemies of the divine states. It has within it a sense of separation. It can grow into clinging, controlling, and fear.

Center - To move from form to contemplation, from multiplicity to unity, from space to spacelessness, from time to timelessness.

Compassion - One of the four divine states. It is the resonance of our heart with the suffering of another. It is that which dissipates the suffering of others, unchanging it remains secure and calm, it is freed from selfish craving and sees the unbroken stream of tears flowing through life. The enemy of cruelty and wickedness, indirect enemy of passionate grief, and has the ability to discard cruelty and wickedness. A well-balanced mind stays between compassion and sympathetic joy.

Child - Purity, potentiality, innocence, spontaneity, the state free of anxiety. The child is of the soul, the product of the conjunction between the unconscious and consciousness; one dreams of a child when some great spiritual change is about to take place under favorable conditions.

Comparison - One of the near enemies of the divine states. It looks to see if we have more of, the same as, or less than another – creates separation and jealousy.

Cloud of Unknowning - Union with God, not as God is

thought or as God is imagined to be, but as God in his nature. An experience of transcending that leads to discovering one's true self.

Equanimity - One of the four divine states. It is the heart being open to all things, embracing impermanence and the inseparable nature of joy/suffering. It is a state absent of attachment or aversion; it is impartiality that is well balanced between compassion and sympathetic joy. A mind well balanced amid vicissitudes of praise, blame, pain, happiness, gains, loss, repute, and disrepute. A person rooted in insight. The enemy of passion, indirect enemy of callousness, and its presence eliminates clinging and aversion.

Ego - Ideas of self-reference. This is me, this is about me, this matters to me, this means I am together, this validates me.

Five - The representation of the unity of heaven with that of the Magna Mater, the Great Mother.

Forest - Forest-symbolism is complex, but it is connected at all levels with the symbolism of the female principle or the Great Mother. The forest is also a symbol of the unconscious. The forest harbors all kinds of dangers and demons, enemies and diseases. Being lost in the forest or finding a way through it is a powerful metaphor for the terrors of inexperience and the achievement of knowledge — of the adult world or of the self. The forest is unknown, the uncontrolled, the dwelling place of minor divinities and spirits.

Heart - Spiritual illumination, truth, and intelligence. The inner person.

House - The house as home represents different layers of the psyche

Ice - Death of the soul. The rigid dividing line between consciousness and the unconscious.

Indifference - One of the near enemies of the divine states. It is the withdrawal and uncaring that is driven by fear. It is a running away from life. The voice of indifferent withdrawal says, "Who cares, I'm not going to let it affect me."

Journey - An expression of the urgent desire for discovery and change. Hence, to study, to inquire, to seek or to live with intensity through new and profound experiences are all modes of travel. Jung saw traveling as an unsatisfied longing that never finds its goal. The goal is in fact the lost Mother or a flight from the Mother. A true journey is evolution, representing a quest that begins in darkness and seeks the light.

Loving-Kindness - One of the divine states. Learning to love life in all its forms, to love unconditionally without a desire to possess, without selecting, a softened heart. The near enemy of hatred, ill will, and aversion, indirect enemy of greed, and has the ability to quench ill will.

Mindfulness - Keeping one's consciousness alive to the present reality.

Mirror - An instrument of self-contemplation as well as the reflection of the universe.

Moon - The master of women. A circular object that is used for reflective meditation; such as, a dewdrop, a mirror, a pool of water, a moonbeam.

Narcissism - The inability to tolerate unpleasant truths about oneself. A tendency which everyone is subject to as we do not want to admit our lack of substance to ourselves and instead project of image of self sufficiency. The paradox is that this posture keeps us estranged from ourselves and drives us to keep the truth about ourselves at bay. It reflects the internal conflict between a drive to insure a fixed and abiding self and to attach to an external object.

Night - The feminine and the unconscious; an anticipatory state that carries the promise of daylight

Object - Psychological term for all external events, stimuli, people, things that have entered the psyche and has taken root in one's mental realm

Observing Mind - The internal watcher or seer who is felt but never known.

Pity - One of the near enemies of the divine states. To feel sorry for "that poor person over there" as if she were different from us: whereas, true compassion is the resonance of our heart with the suffering of another.

Reconciliation - An act that re-establishes balance.

Room - A symbol of individuality, of private thoughts. A closed room lacking windows may be symbolic of non-communication or a symbol of wholeness, of the idea with no exit. It may suggest supreme intelligence's triumph over birth and death (signified respectively by the doors and windows of the room).

Saldage - A Brazilian word representing a feeling of homesickness for a place one feels is home; yet knows cannot be.

Seed - A symbol of the latent and nonmanifest forces that offers hope for reconciliation.

Seven - Symbolic of a cycle completed, of perfect order.

Shadow - The shadow is the negative "double" of the body, or the image of its evil side. The primitive and instinctive side of the individual.

Sin - To miss the mark.

Sophia - Woman as spiritual guide. The intermediary between the soul and the world and ideas.

Stone - Symbol of being, of cohesion, of harmonious reconciliation with one's self. The stone when whole tells of unity and strength; when shattered it symbolizes psychic disintegration.

Sun - Symbol of the source of life and the ultimate wholeness of humans.

Sympathetic Joy - One of the divine states. The felt joy in the happiness of others, teaches people to seek and find joy within and also to rejoice with the joy of others, brings solace to others. Enemy of jealousy (the energy striving to regain that which is "felt loss", loss of beliefs, ideas, dreams, internalized objects formed to compose self. An aversion to the loss of the fusion with objects internalized to define self and to fill the emptiness within), indirect enemy of exhilaration, and has the ability to eliminate dislike.

Teacher - One who encourages the awareness of that which is known.

Three - The smallest number of a family. One began two; two begat three; and the three begat four, the whole. Synthesis, reunion, resolution, creativity, versatility, omniscience, birth and growth. The Trinity.

Three Keys - The threshold of the unconscious. In legend and folklore, three keys are often used to symbolize a like number of secret chambers full of precious objects. The finding of a key signifies the stage prior to the actual discovery of the treasure, found only after great difficulties.

Veil - Concealment of the truth. A metaphor for illusory existence.

Water - Still water symbolizes meditative insight; the struggles of the psychic depths formulating a clear message comprehensive to the unconscious. The projection of the mother image into the waters endows the viewer with characteristics of The Mother. Intuitive wisdom as water finds its way around obstacles.

Wind - At the height of its activity, wind gives rise to the hurricane that is credited with the power of creation and rebuilding.

SELECT SOURCES

Batchelor, Stephen. *Living with the Devil.* New York, 2004.

_____. *Buddhism Without Beliefs: A Contemporary Guide to Awakening.* New York, 1997.

Beresfors, Brian. (trans.) *Mind Training: Like the Rays of the Sun.* New Delhi, 2002.

Alex Berzin, *The Two Truths,* http://www.talkingbuddhism.com (2005).

Bhikkhu, Thanissaro. *An Angry Person.* 1997.

_____. *The Relaxation of Thoughts.* 1997.

_____. *An Analysis of the Path.* 1976.

_____. *Instructions to Rahula at Mango Stone.* 1995.

_____. (trans.) *Anada Sutta to Ananda* (On Mindfullness of Breathing)

Bowen, M. *Family Therapy in Clinical Practice.* New York, 1978.

_____. "An odyssey toward science" in M. Kerr, *Family Evaluation: An Approach Based on Bowen Theory,* New York, 1988, pp. 3-26.

_____. *"A psychological formulation of schizophrenia"* *Family Systems,* Vol. 2, Number 1, (1995): 17-47.

Brown, F. H. *Reweaving the Family Tapestry: A Multigeneralizational Approach to Families.* New York, 1991.

Buddharakkhita, Archarya. *Metta: The Philosophy and Practice of Universal Love.* 1989.

Bullen, Leonard. *Buddhism: A Method of Mind Training.* PBS, 1995.

Bullock, Clara Fullmer. *More than Tongue Can Tell.* 1960.

Burns, Douglas. *Buddhist Meditation and Depth Psychology.* PBS. 1994.

Casey, Michael. *Sacred Reading: The Ancient Art of Lectio Divina.* Liquior Missouri, 1996.

Chaplin, J. *Dictionary of Psychology.* New York:, 1968.

Chodron, Pema. *When Things Fall Apart.* Boston, 1997.

Corey, G. *Theory and Practice of Counseling and Psychotherapy.* Pacific Grove, GA, 1991.

De Silva, Padmasiride. *An Introduction to Buddhist Psychology.* Landam, MD, 2000.

_____. *Buddhist and Freudian Psychology.* Signapore, 1973.

Freud, Sigmund. *An Outline of Psychoanalysis.* New York, 1949.

Epstein, M. *Going to Pieces Without Falling Apart.* New York, 1998.

_____. *Thoughts Without a Thinker.* New York, 1995.

Fogarty, T. F. "Triangles." in E.G. Pedagast, ed., *The Family Compendium I: The Best of the Family.* New York, 1973-1978.

Gaskell, G.A. *Dictionary of all Scriptures & Myths.* Avenel, NJ, 1950.

Gay, Peter, ed. *The Freud Reader.* New York, 1989.

Gilbert, R. M. *Extraordinary Relationships: A New Way of Thinking about Human Interactions.* Minneapolis, MN, 1992.

Guerber, H.A. *The Myths of Greece & Rome.* London, 1934..

Gurerin, P.J. et. al. *Working with Relationship Triangles.* New York, 1996.

_____. *The Evaluation and Treatment of Martial Conflict.* 1987.

Hall, M. *The Bowen Family Theory and Its Uses.* Northvale, NJ, 1991.

Hesiod, *the Homeric Hymns and Homerica; The Homeric Hymns* V.11.7-32

Hillman, J. *The Soul's Code In Search of Character and Calling.* New York:, 1996.

James, William. *The Principles of Psychology.* New York, 1890.

Kaplin, A. *Jewish Meditation.* New York, 1958.

Katzman, Shoshanna. *Gigong for Staying Young.* New York, 2003.

Kerr. M. *Family Evaluation: An Approach on Bowen Theory.* New York, 1988.

Lerner, H. G. *The Dance of Anger: A Woman's Guide to Changing Patterns of Intimate Relationships.* New York, 1985.

_____. *The Dance of Intimacy: A Woman's Guide to Courageous Acts of Change in Key Relationships.* New York, 1989.

Levine, Peter. *Healing Trauma: A Pioneering Program to Restore the Wisdom of your Body.* Boulder, CO, 2003.

McGoldrick, M. et. al. *Women in Families A Framework for Family Therapy.* New York, 1989.

Moore, T. *Soul Mates.* New York, 1994.

_____. *Care of the Soul.* New York, 1992.

Nathanson, D., ed. *Knowing Feeling.* New York, 1996.

Nhat Hanh, Thick. *Living Buddha, Living Christ.* New York, 1995.

Nichols, M. P. *Family Therapy Concepts and Methods.* New York, 1984.

Nimalasuria, Amanda. *Buddha The Healer: The Mind and its Place in Buddhism.* PBS, 1980.

Nyamaponika, Ven. *Buddhist Dictionary Manual of Buddhist Terms and Doctrine.* PBS, 1988.

Ortega y Gasset, J., in H. Beinfield and E. Korngold, *Between Heaven and Earth A Guide to Chinese Medicine.* New York, 1991.

Papero, D. V. *Bowen Family Systems Theory*. Boston, MA, 1990.

Progoff, Ira. (trans.) *The Cloud of Unknowing*. New York, 1957.

Rogers, Carl. *A Way of Being*. New York, 1980.

Rose, H.J. *A Handbook of Greek Mythology*. New York, 1959.

Russell, B. *A History of Western Philosophy*. New York, 1945.

Schneider, A. & Tarshis, B. *An Introduction to Physiological Psychology*. 3rd ed. New York, 1986.

Thera, Nanamoli. *The Four Sublime States*. PBS, 1998.

_____. *The Practice of Loving-kindness*. PBS, 1990.

_____. *Setting Rolling the Wheel of Truth*. PBS.

Thera, Narada Maha. *A Manual of Abhidhamma*. PBS, 1979.

Thera, Nyanaponika. *The Power of Mindfulness: An Inquiry into the Scope of Bare Attention and the Principal Sources of its Strength*. PBS, 1994.

_____. *The Five Mental Hindrances and Their Conquest*. PBS, 1993.

_____. *Anatta and Nibbana*. PBS, 1986.

_____. *Contemplation of Feeling: The Discourse on the Feelings*. PBS, 1983.

Thera, Sarada Weragoda Ven. *Treasury of Truth*. Twiwan.

Toman, W. *Family Constellation*. New York, 1976.

Rose, H. J. *A Handbook of Greek Mythology*. New York, 1959.

Walker, B. G. *The Woman's Encyclopedia of Myths and Secrets*. Edison, New Jersey, 1996.

Walters, M. et. al. *The Invisible Web Gender Patterns in Family Relationships*. New York, 1988.

Walshe, Ruth. *Buddhist Therapy*. PBS, 1985.

Zweig, C. & Abrams, J., eds. *Meeting the Shadow*. New York, 1991.